Creating Space

Some thoughts about reaching out, relating to, and redeeming the lives around you

JON R. ROEBUCK

© 2019

Published in the United States by Nurturing Faith Inc., Macon GA,
www.nurturingfaith.net.

Library of Congress Cataloging-in-Publication Data is available.

ISBN 978-1-63528-076-0

Dedication

This book is dedicated to Dr. Bob Fisher, President of Belmont University, who offers me creative space each day to develop effective faith leaders.

Contents

Introduction

Consider the following scenario: You, along with three friends, agree to meet for lunch at a local restaurant. The hostess asks, "Table for how many?" Because there are four of you, you instinctively ask for a table around which four people can sit. There are four chairs, four sets of silver, and four glasses of water. It's a quaint, personal moment that engages the four of you in good conversation, deepening dialogue, and enduring friendship.

And then it happens. A fifth friend walks into the same restaurant. He is seemingly alone, probably there to grab a quick bite. But as soon as you see him, you wave him over and ask him to join the group. In a quick moment, another chair is pulled from a distant table; another set of silver is obtained; glasses, plates, and chairs are all shifted in order to make room for the newcomer. Within seconds, space has been created—and not just physical space. By welcoming your friend to the table, you have invited him to join the conversation. By including him in the conversation, you have also invited him into a relationship. The physical space leads to relational space, and perhaps even into a deeper redemptive space.

To push the scenario a bit further, let's pretend the newcomer seems "a little off his game." You notice that he hasn't shaved in a day or two, his clothes are ruffled and wrinkled, and there are dark rings under his eyes. You don't want to blurt out, "Man, what's wrong with you?," but you and all the others are thinking that very thought. As the meal lingers and the conversation progresses a little longer, he begins to tell his story. What begins as a normal and matter-of-fact conversation soon erupts into an emotional outburst. He has suffered a job loss. He's been out of work for almost two weeks but leaves the house each morning, pretending nothing is wrong. He doesn't know how to tell his wife. He doesn't know where the money will come from to pay the mortgage. He's afraid of losing everything. He needs help.

Later, once the meal has been consumed and everyone has gone their separate ways, you sit alone in your car and try to process what you have heard from your friend. In your reflection, you wonder how best to help, who needs to be in the loop, and what kind of prayers should you offer on his behalf. Hopefully, due in part to the shared conversation, your friend will find his way through the difficult chapter in his life. With time and intentionality, maybe you can act as a redemptive resource in his story. You can't shake the moment you have just experienced from your mind—and you really don't want to. Compassion, friendship, and human decency will not allow you to let your friend languish without your help.

Step back and think about the power of created space. Because physical space was created, conversational space was allowed to grow. And then with the conversation, the relationship deepened, and the protective walls around your friend's heart began to tumble by the power of kinship, warmth, and concern. A friend who was struggling to the point of desperation left the restaurant with a little more hope and the promise of redeeming friendship. It's what happens when we create space.

Go back to the beginning of all things. I mean the beginning of *all* things—those initial moments of creation when God called the world into being. The book of Genesis records it this way:

In the beginning God created the heavens and the earth. The earth was formless and empty, and darkness covered the deep waters. And the Spirit of God was hovering over the surface of the waters. Then God said, "Let there be light," and there was light. And God saw that the light was good. Then he separated the light from the darkness. God called the light "day" and the darkness "night." And evening passed and morning came, marking the first day. Then God said, "Let there be a space between the waters, to separate the waters of the heavens from the waters of the earth." And that is what happened. God made this space to separate the waters of the earth from the waters of the heavens. God called the space "sky." And evening passed and morning came, marking the second day. Then God said, "Let the waters beneath the sky flow together into one place, so dry ground may appear." And that is what happened. God called the dry ground "land" and the waters "seas." And God saw that it was good. (Gen 1:1–10 NLT)

There is certainly more to the story, but you get the point. God created space from chaos. He chose to carve out space for all living things. He created space for the sun, moon, and stars. He created space for the oceans to form and for the dry land to appear. He created space for plants to flourish, for animals to roam, and yes, even for man to dwell. And in his image we are gifted with the ability to create space for all living things, including people who may not always feel included in our space or in God's. We have the ability to make space for things to happen, for lives to thrive, for relationships to bloom, and for people to find wholeness.

Whether or not we realize it, we have all participated in the creation of space. Years ago, my wife and I made the decision to finish our basement. We added walls, then paint, then carpet, then bookshelves, and finally furniture. We took unused square footage and created space for friends to stay over, for kids to hang out, and for the family to grow. Or consider this, an old chapel at a former church, characterized by moldy carpet, hard pews, and a failing air-conditioning system, saw little use—maybe fewer than five occasions each year. The decision was made to reclaim and renovate the space. Flexible seating was added. New carpet covered the floor. A stage was added, along with special lighting. A projector and screen were installed. Suddenly, the space came to life and quickly became one of the most frequently used rooms in the church. The creation of space can happen anywhere. Several years ago, I remember riding in the back of a rickety pickup truck along the side of a mountain in Haiti. Our team was providing medical relief to some impoverished areas. As we traveled, we passed a couple weary men. We stopped. They hopped in. We created space. We learned that one of them had a sick wife who needed care. Our team stopped and provided a little triage in their small house.

You have done the same thing. You have created room in your home to meet changing family needs. You have carved out space from the chaos of a cluttered garage or an overstuffed closet. You have trimmed back the hedges and added a new deck. You have built a porch or bought a bigger car to accommodate the growing family. But more importantly than simple physical space, you have also created relational space in your life for others to inhabit. You have welcomed others into your conversations. You have included them in your circle of friends. You have invited them over for dinner. At least, I hope you have. Creating space is a creative act that God ordains and authorizes us to do. It doesn't happen by accident. It doesn't happen without cost or time or intentionality. But when we dare to create space, the world changes, and God's kingdom moves forward.

This book is all about the kinds of space every God-follower is called to create. At the heart of this narrative is the description of five spaces we have the ability to create, which become inclusive, significant, and transformative in the lives of others and in our lives as well.

1. *Physical space* is actual space for people to engage and enter our lives. Like pulling up another chair to the table, we must look for ways to make sure there is plenty of room for others to gather in close proximity to us.

2. *Conversational space* is the result of physical space. We live in a cloistered world where people have forgotten the importance of talking with others—even those with differing opinions, viewpoints, and perspectives. There is a vast need for conversational space that is sane, rational, and civil. Rarely do such adjectives describe interactions on social media. And rarely do such conversations occur without intentionality. Conversations develop into relationships.

3. *Relational space* is where things get a little deeper. In relationships, trust is established, emotions are validated, opinions are valued, pain is poured out, and longings are given expression. Such "relational equity" leads to the fourth space.

4. *Redemptive space* is healing space. It allows for the creation of wholeness, for the restoration of that which is broken, for the acceptance of those who have been marginalized, and for the forgiveness that heals. Redemptive space welcomes the wayward, forgives the sinner, and proclaims the self-worth of every person.

5. *Reflective space* is the private space that we need to carve out for ourselves. Each of us needs time to meditate, reflect, ponder, wonder, and rest. We need time for our thoughts to meander a little. We need the space to ask ourselves, "What does this mean? How does this impact my life? What is God seeking to do in this place? What does he want me to do with this moment?"

I once read about a nomadic African tribe that continually traveled in search of shelter, water, and vegetation for their livestock. After a week of walking endlessly, they would stop for a day to, as they stated, "allow their spirits to catch up with them." The same thought is reflected in David's heart when he writes, "He leads me beside quiet waters. He restores my soul" (Ps 23:2–3 NASB). Reflective space is all about introspection, growth, and wisdom. It's the quiet space where we learn, reflect, and mature.

I invite you to join me in this God-ordained quest to create space in our world. Let's create space for the outsider, the marginalized, the left out, the left over, the lonely neighbor, the frightened co-worker, the political adversary, the non-believer, the skeptic, the bruised, the broken, the seeker, the stranger, the isolated, the curious youth, the set-in-her-ways senior adult, the former churchgoer, the abused, the forgotten, the foreigner, the gruff old man, the gun-rights guy, the pro-choice crusader, the Democrat, the Republican, and anyone one else you can get to come along. Let's create space and watch the ways in which the spirit of the living Lord brings transformation, conversation, communication, understanding, and, yes, even love to the table.

Chapter One

Physical Space

∽

From the beginning of time, God has initiated the creation of relationships. The first eleven chapters of Genesis tell the story of God's interaction with all of humanity, beginning with the story of the first family. In chapter 12 the narrative narrows to the story of one family, that of Abram, and the way in which God will establish a covenant with his descendants. God clearly longs to create relationships between himself and his children, and he rejoices when meaningful relationships are made between fellow human beings. But sometimes we don't allow the spirit of God to build a bridge of relationship between ourselves and others because we fail to create the physical space needed for that to happen. We keep people at arm's length. We put distance between ourselves and those with whom we disagree. We separate. We segregate. We cloister ourselves away. We tend to create a homogeneous, small group around our lives defined by people who look like we look, think like we think, talk like we talk, and vote like we vote. And it seems to get worse all the time.

Consider, for example, what has happened in our local neighborhoods. Years ago, houses were constructed, by and large, with big front porches. Family and friends gathered in the evenings to do life together. Meals were shared. Kids played in the yard. Passersby were greeted with a wave, whether they were strangers or lifelong friends.

Neighbors sat on the steps and chatted for a while. There was physical space for neighbors to interact with each other.

But things are different now. Hardly anyone hangs a swing in the tree growing in the front yard. Playsets are built in the backyard, no longer easily accessible to others. Houses are no longer built with large front porches. Instead, decks are built in the back of the house, surrounded by tall fences that keep others out. The only glimpse you might get of a neighbor is in that millisecond when the garage door rises in the morning and the car dashes out into the street. At the end of the day, it's the same thing—the car approaches, the garage opens and quickly closes. There is no sharing of space, conversation, or life. Several years ago, I challenged my church members, during a preaching series on "neighboring," to draw a map of their neighborhood with the closest eight houses represented. I then asked them to write in the first and last names of their neighbors. Few could even come close.[1]

But this idea of creating space is not limited to a discussion of our neighborhoods. It's more about our world. Can we create space for others? Can we welcome someone who is different? Do we make room in our lives for a dissenting opinion, a different faith perspective, or a different ethic formed by someone's very different life experience? Somewhere there has to be a meeting space—a place where civility, respect, humanity, and decency all converge. Some conversations are so difficult, or so delicate, or need to be so nuanced that unless we are willing to do the hard work of creating space for others to join us, those conversations won't happen.

One of my favorite places to eat in Nashville is a place called Arnold's, down on 8th Avenue South. It's a country kitchen kind of place that has a lot of really good food, all cooked the way my grandmother used to cook. If you ever get down there, try the roast beef and the mashed potatoes. You'll thank me.[2] Recently, Arnold's expanded its dining room to accommodate more people. Probably good for business, but it certainly changed one of the dynamics. In the past, as you waited in the buffet line to get your food, you constantly scanned the crowded dining room to see if you would have a place to sit. In keeping with true Southern hospitality, if only two people were sitting at a table for four, it was not considered rude to ask if you could join the table. Suddenly, complete strangers became acquaintances. You never knew whom you might meet or the conversations you might have around a table. I've discovered that a lot of "kingdom of God" conversations can happen around a table, where people agree to act like adults and keep their minds open to the moment. It's one way we can create space.

Jesus had a knack for creating space. He welcomed the stranger, befriended the downcast, affirmed the infirmed, and ate with all kinds of people. He wasn't afraid of social mores or cultural convention. He saw people as human beings to love and not as objects of disdain. Take, for example, the call of Matthew:

> After that He went out and noticed a tax collector named Levi sitting in the tax booth, and He said to him, "Follow Me." And he left everything behind, and got up and began to follow Him.

> And Levi gave a big reception for Him in his house; and there was a great crowd of tax collectors and other people who were reclining at the table with them. The Pharisees and their scribes began grumbling at His disciples, saying, "Why do you eat and drink with the tax collectors and sinners?" And Jesus answered and said to them, "It is not those who are well who need a physician, but those who are sick. I have not

come to call the righteous but sinners to repentance."
(Luke 5:27–32 NASB)

Empowered by the Roman government to collect tax money, tax collectors were notoriously shrewd and dishonest. They were able to collect any amount they wanted to collect because of the authority given to them by the Romans. They often scammed even their own people out of "extra" money. To be a tax collector was to be a horrible person, despised by many. To be a "rich" tax collector was to be an extraordinarily horrible person, despised by all.

So, at least with tax collectors, Jesus knew how important it was to create and inhabit physical space. With Matthew (often referred to as Levi), Jesus not only invited him to follow but welcomed the chance to dine with him in his home. The physical space created previously unimaginable conversations. Matthew would go on to become one of the twelve disciples, and his name would grace the Gospel written by his hand. For Jesus to create the space required the unexpected. He was willing to enter the space of the sinner. He was willing to offer friendship to someone despised by his culture. He was willing to endure the scorn of his critics, because the space was that important. Physical space opened the door to all kinds of other space.

Remember the day that 5,000 people came to hear Jesus preach? He fed them not only with kingdom words, but with the fish and loaves. It's the only miracle of Jesus recorded in all four Gospel accounts. It must have been a day like no other. It began with a small gathering—just Jesus and his disciples, whom he had sent out to proclaim the kingdom and to heal diseases. They had withdrawn to Bethsaida for a time of solitude and reflection, but suddenly their whereabouts were known to all. People poured into the region and gathered on the hillside. And notice what happened next: "But the crowds were aware of this and followed Him; and welcoming them, He began speaking to them about the kingdom of God and curing those who had need of healing" (Luke 9:11 NASB).

It's easy to miss a significant detail in that single verse. With not a care about the interruption of his dialogue with the disciples, *Jesus welcomed* them into his space. In so doing he welcomed them into his presence, his conversation, his teaching, and his kingdom. It was as simple as saying, "You're welcome here. Why don't you join us? Why not take a seat and live in the moment?" It's what happens when we allow for the creation of physical space. Whenever we allow others to enter into our space, we, in effect, invite them into our lives. It has to be an intentional invitation. We create the space, and we welcome others to fill that space.

Or what about the story of the woman at the well recorded in John 4? Jesus, along with the disciples, is traveling from Judea to Galilee. In order to complete the journey, they have to pass through the region of Samaria. Any good Jew would avoid the region if at all possible. Even though it was a much more direct route between the south (Judea) and the north (Galilee), many would choose to traverse a trans-Jordan route just to avoid any possible contact with the despised, half-breed, corrupted Samaritans. The story plays out this way:

> He left Judea and went away again into Galilee. And He had to pass through Samaria. So He came to a city of Samaria called Sychar, near the parcel of ground that Jacob gave to his son Joseph; and Jacob's well was there. So Jesus, being wearied from His journey, was sitting thus by the well. It was about the sixth hour.

> There came a woman of Samaria to draw water. Jesus
> said to her, "Give Me a drink." For His disciples
> had gone away into the city to buy food. Therefore
> the Samaritan woman said to Him, "How is it that
> You, being a Jew, ask me for a drink since I am a
> Samaritan woman?" (For Jews have no dealings with
> Samaritans.) (John 4:5–9 NASB)

It is important to notice a couple things. First, Jesus dared to venture into the territory of people who would not have necessarily welcomed his presence. Though the Jews and the Samaritans shared a common ancestry and faith, the events that played out during the time of the Jewish exile made them bitter enemies. There was some risk and a lot of intentionality about Jesus's decision to stop, rest, and drink from the well at Sychar. Second, Jesus dared to speak to a Samaritan woman publicly. The protocol of the day did not allow for a man to address a woman in public; it was considered shameful. But to speak to a Samaritan was even worse. And notice the time of day: The noonday hour—in the heat of the day—was not the normal time of day to draw water. Instead, water was drawn in the cool of the morning or in the shadows of the late afternoon. The only reason she would have come at such an hour was to avoid the jeers and curses of her fellow citizens who knew of her past and of her current, sinful lifestyle. Certainly, she never would have expected such a moment to occur.

But read the text carefully. Wearied from his journey, Jesus was already seated when she approached the well. The space was his to control because he was there first. As a Jewish rabbi, seated at the well, Jesus held the keys to access and acceptance. He could have ordered her to leave, but he opened the space and initiated a conversation. Dumbfounded, she wondered, "Why would you talk to me?

Why would you ask me to draw water for you to drink?" A lot can happen when physical space is offered and accepted.

You perhaps know how the story progresses: Jesus taught the woman about "living water," the kind of water that sustains life eternally. Having found renewal and redemption, she rushed to the village to tell others, and "many of the Samaritans believed in Him because of the word of the woman who testified, 'He told me all the things that I have done'" (John 4:39 NASB).

What constitutes physical space, and how can we create it? Let's focus on three areas: the local church, the community, and the workplace. Of all places, surely the local church should be the place where civility, respect, and friendly dialogue occur. The local church ought to reflect the spirit of the living Lord, who welcomed sinners into his presence, sought to heal the broken, and allowed those who disagreed with him to at least have a voice. The church could become the best place on earth for critical issues to be discussed. The church could provide the context for meaningful dialogue, peaceful discussion, and redemptive conversation. But is there room for such interplay to occur? In most cases not. The inability of the church to provide physical space is caused by her unwillingness to be intentional about the creation of such space. Until churches and leaders open their minds and doors to the world around them, destiny-altering, life-changing, community-transforming space will not appear. If churches really care about spreading the gospel, they must be willing to allow those who haven't yet responded to that gospel to find a place at their table of welcome.

Consider for a moment some of the conversations swirling around today's culture. Many are divisive, challenging, potentially corrosive, but critically important. Also consider where most of those conversations occur. Many take place in the "free-wheeling, anything-goes" space of social media. Rarely are the conversations civil, helpful, or even factual. Most people want to spew their thoughts and hear only from others who tend to agree with them. There is little space for tolerance, mediation, or respectful discourse. In fact, most of us know people who are stepping away from social media because they are tired of all the negativity, caustic rhetoric, and childish pettiness.

Some of the conversations are happening on the twenty-four-hour news cycles. Most of the news organizations fill the screen with a panel to discuss key topics. While the panels may reflect some diversity in terms of thought and opinion, rarely do they add any meaningful content to our minds. In fact, several news organizations have become so polarizing that it has become difficult to separate fact from fiction. "Fair and balanced" reporting is a quaint notion that was abandoned years ago. The same scenario is played out on talk radio. We tune in to stations with the hosts who think like we do, rarely creating space for a differing opinion. We don't tune in to learn anything new; we tune in to reinforce what we already have concluded.

So where should we go to talk of politics, or racism, or immigration, or addiction, or abuse, or human trafficking, or any other difficult conversation? What if the local church became the "safe place" where thoughts could be honestly expressed, meaningfully discussed, and respectfully considered? I'm not talking about the gossip sessions that often occur in the Sunday school classroom where people gather to study the Bible but really meet just to pontificate and flex their political opinions. I'm not talking about corridor conversations where members feel it's appropriate to take potshots at leaders or their spouses. I'm not talking about Wednesday night prayer meetings where many spread gossip or grandstanding opinions under the guise of "sharing prayer concerns." I am talking about the intentional hosting of meaningful and yet difficult conversations.

Can the church lead the way in creating space that is safe, civil, well-informed, and rational?

The answer is yes. It must be done with intentionality and a lot of hard work behind the scenes. Members have to be willing to play by the rules of respectful dialogue. Members have to be willing to invite others to sit across the table who radically disagree with their own opinions. Members have to remember that no conversation or expression of thought has the authority to usurp the ethic of Christ-like love. Creating space means opening the building and letting others in. It means a willingness to say to anyone and everyone, "You are welcome to come to the table and sit with me a while."

I have a friend who is a Jewish rabbi who role modeled this creation of space for me. Understand that as a Jewish congregation, his flock deals with hatred, prejudice, and anger in ways that most of us can't even begin to imagine. In fact, I asked him recently this simple question: "How often do you have to deal with hate mail?" His response was simple, short, and stunning. "Every day," he replied. "Every day." Even in the midst of a congregation with much to fear and defend, he has found a way to create space for others. I have been invited to speak at the temple on numerous occasions, and each time I have been graciously received. The rabbi even invited me to join him at his home for the Seder meal. I remember thinking at the time, "How could I have been fifty-five years old before I was ever invited to a rabbi's house for a Seder meal?" And then it dawned on me: "How could I have gotten this old without ever inviting a Jewish friend into my home?" But I digress. His congregation is willing to welcome people of other faith traditions, other opinions, and other priorities. It has only enriched their experience and has in no way threatened their belief system.

Creating physical space in a church setting means just that—the church creates a space, a room, a meeting, a meal, a table. It says,

"You are welcome here. Come in, and let's talk." More churches need to see themselves as the answer and not as a fearful cloister of folks who attempt to exclude the world from their space. What if the church, your church, began a block party tradition that welcomed people without qualification to come and eat and talk? What if your church began an interfaith dialogue? What if your church invited local politicians from both sides of the aisle to come and discuss key issues? What if your church adopted a refugee family? What if your church hosted a conference on race? What if your church hosted a meal for marginalized minorities to sit down with elected officials and representatives from local law enforcement agencies? What if your church created a moment where transgender folks were honored as guests just so those members who live with ambiguity and confusion over that issue could at least gain some perspective? What if your church created a safe place for immigrant families to worship, fellowship, and find their footing? It's odd—most churches have so much space within their walls but have so little room to talk. Creating such space will not threaten the values, doctrine, or security of any church; it will only make such things more inclusive, welcoming, relevant, and Christ-like.

Such space is never created without intentionality. Churches don't just stumble upon the idea of creating space. It takes effort. It takes the will to create it. It takes church leaders who are willing to take on the criticism such action inevitably creates. Either we model the welcoming, accepting, and redeeming love of Christ, or we shut our doors to the world around us and hold hands while the numbers diminish and the Spirit dissipates. Creating space doesn't harm the witness of the church, nor water down its message, nor corrupt its doctrine. It establishes it in the community as a place of healing, celebration, and grace.[3]

Now let's talk of creating physical space within the community in which we live or work. Let's start with the work environment. Of course, there can be no "one-size-fits-all" description of what creating space will resemble in the workplace, but here are a few ideas to consider. First, be aware of the physical barriers that lead to isolation and loneliness. Depending on the setting, you may work in a cluster of offices or cubicles where there is constant interaction and dialogue with others. You may interact with others throughout the day. But such a scenario is not always the case. For example, you may work in a setting where individuals work in small offices, in front of screens, with doors always closed. Certainly such a setting provides for great concentration and the ability to get a lot done, but it does little for creating space and dialogue. What it does create is the inability to gain perspective or opinion from others. Walls and doors do exactly what they are intended to do; they keep others out or at least at arm's length. So look for the barriers. What separates and isolates others in your work setting? Can you do anything to alleviate that?

I work in such a setting. And the problem is that I am a "people person." I like the interaction. I crave contact. I want the friendly disruption that relationship-building provides. Therefore, I have adopted an "open-door" policy—unless, of course, I have a private phone call to make, an important one-on-one conversation to host, or if I am bumping up against a deadline and need to crank out a lot of content. But I have found that simply having an open door creates a physical space that is often the beginning of conversational and relational space.

Second, look for ways of inviting others into the space that you long to create. Creating physical space often requires more than just opening a door or providing an empty chair. It involves attitude, the right body language, willingness to risk interaction, maybe a friendly smile. You need to convey a message that says, "I'm glad you're here. You are welcome in this space."

Let me give you a simple example: The custodial staff on the campus where I work includes numerous ethnicities and nationalities. The woman who cleans my office and empties out my trash each day is from Nepal. She is quite shy and unassuming. There are language barriers and cultural differences. But I wanted to create space for her, so I did two things. First, I learned her name, which I am careful to use in every interaction. Second, I took the time to Google a few things about her culture and nation of origin. I wanted to greet her in a friendly way, so I learned a few Nepalese phrases and words. The first time I tried one out on her, she all but dropped her cleaning supplies! She stared for a moment with a sense of wonder on her face and then blurted out a couple sentences in her native language. I had to explain that I only knew a couple words and just wanted to say hello in a way that would welcome her into the space. But you get the point. Open the space with attitude, warmth, and genuine acceptance.

I have also noticed that people are sometimes hesitant to actually step into someone's space or office. They may stand at the door but never feel the freedom or acceptance to actually step in or even sit down. Inviting others into the space you create may mean a handshake along with a word of invitation, asking that person to enter and even sit for a while. It's common sense coupled with common decency.

Third, risk delving into the unknown. Most of us connect with others at work on a surface level. We might wave, offer a word of greeting, and talk about the success of the local sports team, but rarely do we create space that goes beyond the surface. Creating physical space may simply mean that you set your office as the location for your next meeting. You invite others into your space.

It may mean risking a lunch conversation. Saying "Let's meet for lunch in the cafeteria" may be a positive way to create physical space that is non-threatening. Maybe your environment lends itself to the possibility of taking a brief walk or stopping for a cup of coffee. There are so many things to learn from others that we will never know because of our inability or unwillingness to create physical space for dialogue to occur. Don't get me wrong. You don't want to be "that annoying guy" whom people hate to see coming their way. Creating space does not mean creating an annoyance. You have to use your common sense and read the "vibes" that people are throwing off. But do consider the creation of physical space where interaction, conversation, and sharing can occur.

A couple years ago I had the privilege of meeting Jim Morgan, who served as the chairman and CEO of Krispy Kreme Doughnuts, Inc., from 2005–2016. Many give Jim credit for rescuing the company from financial collapse and bankruptcy. When he took over the company, he put a number of policies and initiatives into place to build morale, teamwork, and financial accountability. He also created space. Jim is a committed Christian and wanted to infuse a "take your faith to work" mentality at his company without being coercive or discriminatory. So he simply dedicated a room— an actual physical space—within the confines of the building where religious groups could meet for Bible studies, prayer, or other meaningful religious observances. Any faith tradition was invited to use the space. There were no restrictions or limits. He discovered that simply creating space provided for healthy and open dialogue among employees of various faith traditions. It was good for the company and good for the kingdom as well.

Finally, let's consider creating physical space in the community where you live. Maybe it begins with a willingness to create a space in your own home where visitors are welcome, where food is shared, where conversations happen, and where relationships deepen. The problem with our "home space" is that most of us are not comfortable welcoming strangers. We don't mind entertaining the extended family, or our small group, or even a few neighbors, but to invite people of a different culture, race, nationality, or political understanding is asking quite a lot. (I'm a lifelong, dyed-in-the-wool University of Alabama fan. It gets challenging when my wife's family arrives with all of their Auburn apparel!) But until we are willing to open the door to potential relationships, we will insulate ourselves within our own homes. In so doing, we will miss the blessing of mind-expanding, relationship-deepening, redemption-creating conversations. Our perspectives will remain shallow, and our circles will continue to be very limited and small. Creating physical space literally entails opening the door of your home. An open door is a welcoming and accepting posture to take.

Another way of creating physical space can occur when you open your garage door and leave it open during a day in which you work in the yard, fix the car, or build something with power tools. I'm serious. There is just something about an open garage, an open hood, or the sound of power tools that is irresistible. Curious minds always want to know what is going on, and it won't take long for someone to drift over. Recently, I set up my table saw in the middle of my driveway, along with a pile of lumber. My goal was to create a couple Adirondack chairs. But what I did unintentionally was create a gathering space for my neighbors to catch up with each other. I even let them sit in the chairs when I completed them.

I have a neighbor who did something really interesting when his kids were younger. Rather than retreat to the privacy of his backyard, he used some long rope and a piece of wood and made an amazing swing—old-school style, tied to a tree, one person at a time, another pushing. Every pleasant afternoon, kids swarmed that old tree. Families were introduced. Stories were swapped. Relationships were formed.

Look for occasions to build community. My cul-de-sac has figured this out without a lot of forethought or planning. Every Fourth of July, someone will set out a grill at the end of their driveway and start cooking burgers and dogs. Someone cooks baked beans, someone else grabs a bag of chips, and someone brings ice and drinks. Before you know it, families spill out into the cul-de-sac to talk, laugh, eat, and share time together. The creation of the physical space makes it happen. The same thing happens every Halloween. Two or three families set up a folding table and spread out all the candy. Someone brings a firepit, and someone else brings out some folding chairs. Pretty soon, a lot of really good community takes place.

Physical space has to be welcoming, non-threatening, inclusive, and intentional. That's why the idea of a driveway get-together may be a much easier way to build inclusion. There are some who will not be comfortable walking into your home but who will enjoy the safe space of the sidewalk. Cookouts and conversations are also a great way for non-traditional family groupings to feel welcome. When your vibe is universally welcoming, it won't take long for people to respond.

Decades ago I came across an idea in one of Anthony Campolo's books (I don't remember the title, but I do remember the idea). He had this notion of creating community by sharing assets. Rather than everyone in the neighborhood having a lawnmower, why not have one in common and take turns using it? Instead of everyone owning an extension ladder, again, why not have one in common and let everyone use it when needed? Instead of two cars in every garage, why not have a car or two for carpooling or for occasional use so people could share the resources once devoted to the second car with those who have needs? You may or may not want to embrace such a radical sharing of goods and wealth, but hopefully you see the point. There are simple steps we can take to create physical space—an open door, a raised garage, an open-ended invitation. Offer a chair to someone looking for a place to sit, and you will create all kinds of space.

This initial step of creating physical space is so fundamental to the process of changing the world around you. It's how relationships and understanding between strangers begin. The concept is simple, but the implementation takes a little effort. As I have already stated, the key word has to be *intentionality*. Don't wait for someone else to create a space. Be the catalyst. Be the energy behind it all. Be the dreamer. Be the visionary. Be the person God uses to build a bridge, make a connection, start a dialogue, and maybe even end some destructive discord.

Endnotes

[1] The genesis behind this idea of drawing a map and naming the people who live close by came from an insightful and inspiring book titled *The Art of Neighboring* (Grand Rapids: Baker Books, 2012). Written by Jay Pathak and Dave Runyon, it offers some great ideas on building genuine relationships. I highly recommend this book as a resource for those who want to think strategically about neighboring as a kingdom-building strategy.

[2] I once took my college-aged daughter to eat there. I said to her, "Keep your eyes open; you might see a country music star." Within moments country music legend Porter Wagner walked in. I poked my daughter and said, "Look! There's Porter Wagner!" She replied, "Who?" Oh well—I tried.

[3] The creation of such space is not without hurdles. Opening the doors of the church to individuals who normally do not fill that space could create moments of tension, misunderstanding, or even conflict. In the midst of becoming a welcoming community, it is important to consider security protocols, guidelines, and boundaries/expectations for behavior. This in no way implies that any or all newcomers will inherently bring with them such issues. It is to say, however, that careful planning and prudence should always be a part of the conversation to ensure a smooth creation of dialogue and interaction.

Chapter Two

Conversational Space

One of the great conversations recorded in the pages of Scripture is found in John 3:1–21 when a Pharisee named Nicodemus comes to Jesus under the cover of darkness to probe his mind, listen to his teaching, and learn about the kingdom. Nicodemus was a Pharisee, a keeper of the Mosaic Law, and a defender of the faith in the first-century Jewish world. Pharisees applied the Mosaic Law to contemporary situations. Their application expanded the Ten Commandments into more than 600 rules and regulations to be applied. Nicodemus is referred to in the text as "a ruler of the Jews" (John 3:1 NASB). He was obviously a man of importance, status, and authority.

Some are quick to point out the secret nature of Nicodemus' journey. He needed the secrecy of the evening shadows to conceal his identity and whereabouts. Other Johannine scholars read even more into the statement. Gospel writer John does a lot with the image of light and dark as he writes. Darkness always refers to a time of evil or to those moments when people are unclear in terms of their understanding of Jesus and to the ways of God. Such a point of view would literally mean that Nicodemus was "in the dark" about Jesus's identity.

Read the text carefully and the setting for the conversation seems a little vague. Verse 2 simply indicates that "this man came to Him

[Jesus] by night" (John 3:2 NASB). One can only presume a couple answers in terms of location. Perhaps Jesus was staying somewhere in the environs of Jerusalem with friends (John 2:23 indicates Jesus was in Jerusalem at the time of the Passover feast). Or perhaps Jesus and his disciples took refuge in the wilderness, resting under the stars as many did when the city swelled to capacity during the feast (the garden of Gethsemane, perhaps?). Or it could even be that Jesus was staying somewhere within the city itself. If so, the explanation of Nicodemus slipping through the shadows makes a lot of sense. But wherever Jesus was found, he clearly had the ability to welcome or shun the presence of Nicodemus. The space was his to control. By receiving Nicodemus into his physical space, Jesus created conversational space.

And what a conversation it was. Ideas were discussed, teaching offered, honest questions asked and answered. The concept of being born again into eternal life moves to the forefront. Salvation (not judgment) enters the equation as Jesus proclaims God's love and his intention for saving humanity. The conversation was eye-opening, mind-bending, and life-changing for Nicodemus. It is a reminder that only when people actually talk, engage in conversation, and explore new thoughts and ideas does the seed of relationship, healing, and redemption get planted. It's all about a conversation.

I was in college in the late seventies and early eighties. I attended Samford University in Birmingham, where I studied religion and learned about ministry. I was also a proud member of Sigma Nu fraternity. In those fraternity relationships I learned a lot about choices and perspectives on life that were vastly different from my own. My two closest friends on the planet were a part of that experience with me. They are the best of men, and they have made me a better man because I know them. In those days Sigma Nu had a fierce rivalry with Pi Kappa Phi. We competed about everything from grade point averages, to intramural sports, to girlfriends, to StepSing trophies. It was a bitter competition that, in all honesty, probably made both groups work harder at excelling.

I remember the year I was a Sigma Nu pledge. Our pledge class meetings were held on Sunday evenings at the frat house. One of the traditions each week was to go outside, face the Pi Kapp house (which was next door), and yell, "Give up!" We did that week after week after week. We were rivals. We thought about things differently. We competed. We ignored each other in most social settings. And in those years we did very little talking to each other. Oh, we were civil most of the time when in public, but we weren't connected in any real way.

I've often wondered what we missed by not talking. I'm sure there were great friendships that were never formed and ideas that could have helped us all that were never expressed. And there were probably great and noble causes in the city to be undertaken for the common good if we had just learned to communicate. But there was no shared physical space; thus, there was no conversational space.

Someone once said that ninety percent of the world's problems are problems of communication. There's a lot of truth in that thought. We need to talk. We need to talk about things both great and small. We need to talk about shared vision and opposing ideals. We need to talk about problems and their solutions. We need to talk about cultural differences, political divides, and difficult societal issues. We need to give ourselves space for civil, rational, intelligent, and peaceful words. Until we talk, relationships will never begin, and important issues will never find a common ground of understanding.

The problem is that there are very few places in our cultural context for such conversations to occur. For example, if you wanted to discuss the political dissonance of our day in a peaceful, relaxed, informative, and sane manner, where would you go? Talk radio is not the place; it's too one-sided, too inflamed. A local political rally is not the place; only one viewpoint is expressed. Social media is not the place; too many opinions come from anonymous "ranters." The neighborhood church is not the place; there's too much fear that someone might get offended. The local bar is not the place; people come there to relax, not argue about politics and religion, right? The neighborhood block party is not the place; the desire to live in peace with neighbors forbids any conversation about divisive matters. The local high school football game is not the place; who wants the tension between people who have to sit close to each other week after week?

You get the point. Conversational space is difficult to create and perhaps even more difficult to manage or control. Where do you talk about politics? Where can you talk about religious beliefs? Where do you go to talk about immigration or racism or addiction or human trafficking? Until there is physical space, there will be no conversational space. And if there is no intentionality about creating either, things will never change.

Several years ago, I was hosting a planning committee dedicated to the task of designing a Diversity Day experience for a program called LeadershipNashville. LeadershipNashville is an ongoing program that creates a yearly cohort of thirty or so leaders who spend a year together learning about the dynamics of the city. The group I hosted was quite diverse. There were various races, ethnicities, nationalities, and religions represented. Because I held the planning meeting at the church where I was serving as pastor, there were some who didn't want to enter a Christian setting and chose not to attend. I also discovered that some had never been in a "white" church before. I learned not to seat the Muslim gentleman next to the Hindu gentleman. I was certainly struck by the irony that there was such deep-seated division on the planning team to coordinate Diversity Day! Heaven help us all.

Therefore, we must intentionally think about creating physical space for the purpose of creating meaningful dialogue. It's not enough just to gather folks around the table. Someone has to ensure that conversation is welcoming, opinions are heard, viewpoints are balanced, and a spirit of friendship permeates the moment. That "someone" needs to be a recognized leader who is fair, authentic, wise, and trusted. Sometimes the best agenda for such a gathering is to have no agenda. Fill the space with diverse people, and let them learn from each other. There is something important about gathering people of diverse thought together in ways that normal life doesn't provide. Make the space and the time for conversations to happen. But manage the moment well. Make sure the conversation doesn't get off the rails or become too one-sided.

Though some may express reluctance to hosting such a conversation because of a "church-and-politics-don't-go-together" mentality, the local church may well be the very best place for such conversations to occur. The point is not to preach, push a political agenda, postulate a position on a divisive topic, or claim moral superiority. The point is to allow people a safe place just to talk about things that matter. What if the neighborhood church became known in the community as that safe place where people could go to hear balanced conversations and differing perspectives? Can the church allow conversations that matter to happen within its space? It can, and it must.

I love the town hall meeting format. Gather folks for a meal. Let them share space and conversation. Let them hear and respond to each other. Agree upfront that everyone is welcome and that no one has the right to be overbearing, mean-spirited, or angry. To be sure, some conversations have to be carefully nuanced by a skilled leader.

But don't let fear about what could go wrong keep you from hosting a conversation about what needs to be made right. The problem with many of our "thorny" issues is that a lack of created space forces such conversations to stay within the confines of those "thought islands" where we only talk to people whom we know agree with us or in places where we don't have to listen to any dissenting voices. We may as well just talk to ourselves and get angry at the rest of the world for not seeing things the way we do.

In my work at Belmont University with the Reverend Charlie Curb Center for Faith Leadership, I host periodic breakfast conversations about some difficult topics. These conversations are limited in two ways. First, only twenty-five people participate. I want people to literally sit around a table so they can meet, dialogue, and learn from each other. The other limitation is time. These conversations, including the mealtime, are limited to two hours. This tends to keep the conversation focused and moving along. Sometimes, as the executive director of the program, I lead the conversation. At other times, when the topic needs more expertise, I invite an expert to make a brief presentation. From time to time, I also employ the use of a panel to aid in our understanding. I insist that all expressed thoughts and opinions are welcome and that disagreements can never become angry or ugly. To date we have tackled topics like LGBTQ rights, racism, caustic politics, gun violence, immigration, human trafficking, health care as a moral obligation, interfaith issues, gentrification of neighborhoods, and more. These are all topics with which faith leaders wrestle. It just makes sense that we might learn more together than any one of us might learn on our own. The conversational space has built new friendships and new understanding. It's the kind of space that needs to be created in every community (faith communities and local municipalities) to deal with difficult issues. When describing what I do as the director of the center, a friend once said to a questioner, "He creates space." Exactly.

But let's move beyond the need to create space about difficult cultural topics to a discussion of the ways we need to create one-to-one conversational space. Building personal relationships is at the heart of gaining perspective, building goodwill, and finding a better way to relate to each other. Understand my perspective—not every conversation needs to be about a difficult or potentially divisive issue. In fact, most of them don't need to be about such things. It is only in the safe space of a curated relationship that difficult, emotionally charged issues should be discussed. Remember that relational space can only be created over time, over many cups of coffee, or over several shared meals. Conversations about the simple things will become the tools that will create the deeper relationship. For now let's consider how we at least begin the process of talking.

I'm an extrovert—always have been. I can walk up to a stranger and start a conversation about most anything. As my wife likes to say, "Jon has a healthy dose of self-esteem." I know that is not the case for everyone, but starting conversations is easy for me. Where I may stumble is in the willingness to get deep and even expose my own vulnerabilities as relationships grow. So where and how can surface-level communication begin? Again, the key word is *intentionality*. Communication can happen anywhere contact occurs—in the parking lot, at the store, in the workplace, at church. The possibilities are endless. But until you are willing to create the space and the moment for a conversation to occur, not much will change.

Let me draw an illustration from my days of high school chemistry. I took AP chemistry, which included a lot of lab work. I remember the day our teacher, Mr. Dennison, wanted to illustrate a "concussive" reaction. He told us that sometimes two chemicals can be at rest with each other even though they are in contact. But when a force or circumstance causes them to react, then and only then does the chemical reaction occur. To prove his point, he poured out a small amount of two chemicals onto the floor. Nothing happened. But then he introduced a force to combine the two chemicals—in this case a yardstick—and react they did! (He probably should have measured the amounts.) The result was a huge explosion that filled the room with smoke, knocked out a few windows, and blew a hole in the floor! We all went running for the door, and he went running to the employment office to find a new job.

Here's my point: You can live next door to someone, or sit on the same pew, or work on the same hall, or share the same bus, or study at the same school, or walk the same sidewalk for years and never develop any kind of relationship because you never offered a word of conversation. *Intentionally* create a moment. Stop the next time you are walking your dog and ask your neighbor how it's going. Walk down the hall at work and say to that co-worker, "I'm going to grab a coffee. You interested in taking a break?" Or when the service is over, stop that person who sits on your pew and say, "You know, I've have been sitting close to you all of these months and I don't even know your name." Obviously you need to pay attention to the normal cautionary guidelines. Where you meet and when you meet and what you discuss when you do are all important considerations. You never want to create the appearance of something that could be inappropriate. You never want to make someone feel awkward or "put on the spot." But until you are willing to at least risk the initial stages of a conversation, you will remain like those two chemicals described earlier, which can sit side-by-side for a long time and never react in any way.

Let me offer a couple easy and practical suggestions. First, why not push the idea in your neighborhood for that cookout I described earlier? Set the place as your front yard and promise to carry the heavy weight for the meal. Supply the tables and chairs and the burgers. But then ask who would be willing to bring bottled water, or a dessert, or maybe chips. A simple community meal might be the catalyst for some conversation starters. And of course realize that you are planting seeds of relationships. Don't use the meal in a way that seems disingenuous or sneaky. In other words, it's not the time to talk politics or Mary Kay, to hand out business cards or "4 Spiritual Laws" tracts. It's just the time to meet your neighbors and share a few moments together in a non-threatening way.

I have a neighbor who lives behind me whom I don't know very well. I know his first name and where he works, but that's about it. He's single, and any close family members live several states away. But every year he throws a Christmas party in December. He invites friends, co-workers, and neighbors. He tells everyone to bring something to add to the snack table—or just come. And people do. It's an odd mix of people who normally have zero contact or communication. But we sit and talk and laugh, and conversations begin. All it takes is a willingness on his part to create the space by opening his home.

Second, believing that a lot of good conversations begin around a simple meal, why not invite another family over to your home for dinner? If that seems too awkward, then invite two families. Tell them you have no agenda, that you thought it would be nice to get to know them a little better. The key is to create the moment. If you are not comfortable with inviting folks into your home, then agree on a local restaurant. And if part of your agenda is to understand the world from someone else's perspective, then you may want to entertain the idea of inviting a family whose worldview is different—a different race, a different nationality, a different native language.

Conversational space is all about finding the time and place to simply talk. To create such space we have to carve out some time away from work, our phones, or whatever else distracts us long enough to be "fully present" with someone so we can talk, listen, exchange a few words, or express a few thoughts. The goal is to share a little time and life with each other and see what happens in the mysterious space where lives intersect.

Travel back in time to the experience of Moses, when God called him to his life's work while Moses stood in the midst of the Midian Desert (Exod 3). The moment came when eighty-year-old Moses was tending his flock, perhaps leaning on his staff, gazing off into the distant horizon. But something strange and wonderful happened. Suddenly, a small bush burst into flames. And even more unusual, the bush was not consumed by the fire. He took a few steps to draw a little closer. The scriptures tell the story with these words: "When the LORD saw Moses coming to take a closer look, God called to him from the middle of the bush, 'Moses! Moses!'" (Exod 3:4 NLT). In that moment God carved out a physical space to allow himself to enjoy conversational space with Moses. It was not the only conversation the two would share on a mountaintop. In fact, it was the first of many. It was the first step in creating a relationship that would shape, change, and govern the heart of Moses for the next forty years.

Think about it. Every great friendship or relationship begins with a simple conversation. Shared time changes lives. It breaks down barriers. It open doors. Create the physical space, and a conversation will soon follow. Talk long enough, and a relationship will begin to emerge.

Chapter Three

Relational Space

A relationship is different from an acquaintance, a workmate, or even a casual friendship. It goes deeper than that. Relationships are forged on the anvil of time spent in each other's space and in each other's conversations. Relationships form when trust is offered, when walls of separation begin to crumble, and when common interests and thoughts are explored. There is a sense of vulnerability. There is a mutual respect and civility. There is a willingness to step a little further into someone else's life and experience. Even the term itself implies connecting points that did not exist previously. We grow from a casual acquaintance into a relationship. For example, when someone on Facebook changes their status to indicate that they are "in a relationship," it means things have gotten a little more serious, a little more connected. The parameters of the relationship have become a little more defined. Relationships are determined by the way we are connected, joined, or linked to each other. To use the words of the old hymn, relationships describe "the tie that binds" us to one another.

To be sure, there are various levels of relationship. At some moments the levels are defined by limiters like time, space, and interest. We may be in relationship with many people, but certainly some of those relationships are much deeper and much more intense than others. The point of this chapter is not to define how deep every relationship should go, but to simply recognize the fact that if we are willing to do so, we can form healthy, growing, and nurturing connections with other people that can benefit our lives and theirs. The question is whether or not we are willing to allow others in, to create enough room in our lives to share a little "deeper" space.

There are a number of great relationships described in the pages of Scripture. Minds tend to gravitate toward relationships like that of David with Jonathan. These two men were so closely linked in friendship and loyalty that the scripture states, "The soul of Jonathan was knit to the soul of David" (1 Sam 18:1 NKJV). Some relationships have that level of depth. As kids we used to talk about "blood brothers" as we mingled both spit and blood and shook hands to seal the deal. As adults we talk in terms of having a "soulmate" or "best friend." Any of us are truly blessed to have one or two people in our lives who love us unconditionally and who stay connected to us throughout the journey. The story of Moses and Aaron also comes to mind. They were brothers, but beyond that, they were partners in the all-consuming work of God. Moses was the powerful leader who was afraid to speak publicly. Aaron became the speaker for the pair and the supportive right hand of his brother. In their story we see the way God sometimes calls us to enter into the life of another so our weakness might be lessened as we, in turn, fill in the gaps of weakness in that person's life. Other stories of relationship are found in the pages that describe the work of Elijah and Elisha or even the ministry partnership of Timothy and Paul.

One of the great stories of the Bible is the narrative titled after the main character and heroine of the story, Ruth. You may recall that a Jewish man named Elimelech married a woman named Naomi. The couple was blessed with two sons, Mahlon and Kilion. Because of severe famine, the young family moved to the land of Moab to escape scarcity. Once settled in the land, Elimelech died, leaving a grieving widow and two boys. The sons grew and married Moabite women. Ruth and Orpah became members of the family. About a decade later, both Mahlon and Kilion died. Naomi was left in a strange land as a vulnerable widow with two newly widowed women at her side. Naomi encouraged each daughter-in-law to return to her family and to marry again. She kissed them goodbye, and they broke down and wept at the sad moment in their lives. Orpah, with regret, left to return to her birth family. Ruth, on the other hand, refused to depart and promised staggering loyalty to Naomi: "Don't ask me to leave you and turn back. Wherever you go, I will go; wherever you live, I will live. Your people will be my people, and your God will be my God. Wherever you die, I will die, and there I will be buried. May the LORD punish me severely if I allow anything but death to separate us!" (Ruth 1:16–17 NLT). Talk about the unbreakable bonds of a relationship! Ruth had signed on for life. The relationship was characterized by loyalty, self-sacrifice, unconditional love, and lifelong security.

Naomi and Ruth certainly provide a model of a deep and abiding relationship. It's the kind of relationship and commitment any of us would long to know in our own lives. But let me trace how some of the connection was formed. First, Naomi created both physical and emotional space in her life. She made room for her sons' foreign-born wives. As the years rolled along, hundreds, if not thousands, of conversations were exchanged. There would be words of counsel, words of wisdom, words of family tradition, words of advice, words of faith and hope. I am sure that at times there were words of anger, words of uncertainty, perhaps words of judgment. No long-term relationship is exempt from the various dimensions of the human spectrum of emotion. But through the shared space of conversation and thought, relationships formed.

I am not suggesting that every conversation we have with a stranger will morph into the depth of such a relationship. But I am suggesting that with each conversation, the "tie that binds" gets drawn a little closer. I have a connection to another neighbor who lives close by that illustrates how burgeoning relationships are formed over several, if not many, conversations. We've been neighbors for the past seven years, with little or no connection. I know his name, but I don't think he knows mine. We have nodded and waved for years, but I've never been in his home, and he's never been in mine. But we have a connecting point. We both drive Mini Coopers. In fact, he owns two of them—one to drive when the weather is nice and one to drive when there is rain or snow (I kid you not). But it's the connecting point of the cars that has ushered us into each other's lives. We have swapped stories and experiences and shared insights into car maintenance for the past couple years.

A few days ago, there was a knock at my front door. It was my neighbor. It was the first time he had ventured that far into my world. "Are you busy?" he asked. "If you've got a minute, I could use your help over in my garage." I didn't even ask why. I just said, "Sure, let's go." Moments later I found myself in his space, his world, his garage. He needed me to help him put a new door on his car. He found a new door for his car in Florida on a recent vacation and brought it home to install it, because the color matched the original color of his car a little more closely. (It's a long story, and if you are not a car fanatic, you probably wouldn't understand anyway.) But you see the point. We have shared the same neighborhood space for a long time, and with each conversation the buds of a deepening relationship have begun to break through the surface.

I spend a lot of time these days teaching and thinking about ways to develop successful leaders. I recently came across a definition of leadership that was so simple and spot on: "Look around and see if anyone is following you. If they are, then you are a leader. If they are not following you, then you are not a leader." Makes sense, right? Leaders have to have followers. That's what defines leadership. In like fashion, the definition of a relationship can be rather simply stated: "Do you relate to anyone? If you connect with someone else in a meaningful way, then you are in a relationship with that person. If there is no connection, then no relationship can exist."

In this discussion of relational space, it becomes necessary to think about how each of us can position ourselves to build relationships through the conversations we have. What is contained in our casual conversations that sets the foundation for deeper trust and connection? First, we need to become comfortable with the idea of collecting friends along the way. By *collecting* I mean the process by which we first engage, strike up an interest in, and explore the people around us. Recently, I spent some time in the Great Smoky Mountains National Park with my grandchildren. My wife and I enjoyed a week-long vacation with our kids and grandkids, and one of the best times of the trip was hiking in the mountains. My grandkids, like all children, enjoy throwing sticks into the local creeks and watching the current move them along. As we hiked together, we spent a lot of time collecting sticks and twigs. Once we gathered a sufficient amount, we headed to water's edge to begin the process of tossing and watching. Keep that image in your mind for a moment. My suggestion of "collecting friends" is not for the purpose of holding them for a while only to quickly dismiss them when the fast current of life catches up. That's not the point. The point is once again *intentionality*. We have to be open and willing to enter another person's life and have them enter ours if relationships are going to form. We have to think of what is needed to "collect people" along the way.

For some, making and developing friendships is easy. My friend Mike seems to have a lot of really good friendships. He's a master at welcoming people into his world. He is warm, friendly, gregarious, and engaging. It seems easy for him to find connecting points. He understands how to make people feel comfortable around him and consistently welcomes new thought and perspective. Good for Mike. But I know many others who are not like Mike at all. They struggle to connect with others. They aren't good with the first words of a relationship. They seem a little reluctant to engage others. They have difficulty connecting with people in meaningful ways. Creating physical and conversational space is hard enough, much less creating relational space. Relationships are rarely formed by coincidence or accident. Typically, a little effort goes a long way. Express an interest in someone's world, and they will invite you in.

Second, we need to realize that most relational space is filled by those who take a genuine interest in the lives of others. All people long to be valued, welcomed, and heard. Those who are effective at creating new relationships have learned the value of taking interest in others. They listen to the words spoken, the stories told, the values held, and the pains experienced. Relationship-building often hinges on the listening skills of both people in the relationship. Nothing kills an emerging relationship any faster than someone who dominates each discussion, presses each opinion, and insists on talking more than they listen. Relationships are two-way streets. With the sharing of physical space must come the sharing of emotional, conversational, and reflective space if relationships are going to flourish. People need to look for ways to relate and connect with each other. The superficial and idle chatter of a first conversation can soon develop into real depth and real substance with time.

At Belmont I have a lot of relationships. Some carry great depth and meaning while others are shallow and simple. For example, there are co-workers I occasionally pass in the halls or with whom I occasionally share an elevator ride. We know each other's names and job titles. We have shared a couple elevator conversations about the mundane and common things of life. Sometimes we walk together to the parking garage at the end of the day and chit-chat along the way. But that's about it. A distance remains between us. But on the opposite end of the spectrum, there are several co-workers with whom I share relationships of much greater depth. We've spent time over lunch, on a project, or even on a mission trip. The layers that guard the heart have been peeled away over many conversations and shared moments, and we now live in a true relational space. If we are willing to be vulnerable, open, accepting, and genuinely interested in others; if we are willing to allow someone to step into our world; if we are willing to invest some time, trust will be established, and relationships will grow.

Creating relational space in the life of the local church may be a little harder than you think. Every church out there wants to boast in their warmth, their inclusion of others, and their superior ability to welcome new folks into the life of the congregation. There are greeters in the parking lot, ushers at the door, and volunteers at the information booth to respond to any need. And yet some find it hard to gain an entry point into the life of the church, and here's why. No matter how "open" a group considers itself to be, it becomes a closed group within months, if not weeks. Let me illustrate. Suppose you begin a new small group with some peers at your church. You select a weekly meeting place and time, and off you go. You invite a number of couples, and within a few weeks, a core group of six couples begins to gel as a group. Relationships form. Stories are added to the narrative. Common interests are explored. Without warning, the group becomes closed. To be sure, you don't see it that way, and you sure didn't intend for it to be that way.

But how hard is it for a new couple to now join the group? They are already well behind in being a part of the original DNA of the group. The rest of the group now has a history that the newcomers are trying to overcome. Relational space for the newcomer will be a little harder to create. (The key, by the way, in such a scenario is the creation of more new groups.)

But even though they are hard to create, relationships are the glue that absolutely binds a church together. People may first visit because they like the preacher, enjoy the music, or think the building is attractive. But they will stay because of relationships. Think again in terms of collecting people. Unless your church is willing to allow newcomers in and create space for their thoughts, opinions, and needs, they won't stay for very long. Next Sunday, take a look in the lobby. Look for the people on the fringe, those who are not connected in a relationship with anyone else. Take a close look, because you won't see them again. People will only stand on the outside for so long. Carve out the physical space that is welcoming, inviting, and inclusive. Include the stranger in your conversations. And then listen and share with them long enough until it is clear that a relationship is established.

For a moment let's discuss the creation of relational and conversational space within the "inner workings" of the local church where committees and teams often do the hard work of visioning and planning. It has been my experience that the more people you can invite to the table, the greater the success of any ministry initiative. Churches have a tendency of being fragmented, cliquish, and a little dysfunctional. One way to be more productive and unified is to welcome the concept of collaborative conversation. Conversations in which various viewpoints, suggestions, and opinions are welcome and given value have a way of providing better perspective and greater depth of wisdom. Obviously not every aspect of church life lends itself to collaborative discussion, but whenever church leaders can create the opportunity to invite more people into the conversation, decisions are more broad-based, more carefully considered, and more likely to receive the support of the entire congregation.

According to the Gospel of Luke, on his way to Jerusalem and the events that would unfold as a part of that perilous week we now call Holy Week, Jesus made his way through the nearby town of Jericho. A man named Zacchaeus was hiding in a tree along the route where Jesus and his entourage were to pass. He was in the tree for a couple reasons. First, he simply wasn't tall enough to see Jesus over the heads of people standing in front of him in the crowd. But being short wasn't the real reason he was hiding in the tree. It had more to do with his occupation and reputation. He was a tax collector—a *chief* tax collector—and he was rich. Odds are that he had defrauded nearly every person in the crowd. Though he was from Jericho, he was marginalized by his poor choice of occupation. He was despised and hated by the people of the town. It would not have taken much for a mob mentality to rise up against him.

Luke picks up the story with these words: "When Jesus reached the spot, he looked up and said to him, 'Zacchaeus, come down immediately. I must stay at your house today.' So he came down at once and welcomed him gladly" (Luke 19:5–6 NIV). Jesus created physical space. He made room in the midst of the swaying crowd to give Zacchaeus a safe place in which to stand. And then Jesus indicated that he would stay with Zacchaeus and his family in Zacchaeus's home. It was startling. Unthinkable. Unimaginable. Shocking. But it was glorious from the tax collector's point of view. You see the progression again—physical space led to conversational space. And as the conversation continued, a relationship began—a relationship that led to transformation, healing, and salvation.

The kingdom grows most effectively through relationships. In fact, I've yet to meet a new convert to the faith who didn't come to Christianity apart from a relationship with someone who pointed them in that direction. Relationships become the bridge over which the gospel most often travels. And because that is the case, it becomes critical for churches to promote relationship over ritual, religion, and routine. Churches need to think strategically about creating a welcoming community that invites relationship-building, remembering as they do that there is an ultimate purpose in the creation of that relationship: to introduce friends to the love of Jesus Christ. It is my personal belief that this concept of faith-sharing through relationships is missing in much of twenty-first-century American Christianity. I have visited church after church after church that has relegated the intentional sharing of faith to more of a "I-will-witness-through-my-lifestyle" kind of experience. That's a noble thought, but not an effective strategy. Somewhere along the line, churches need to be clear about why they exist and what the driving priority has to be. There are a lot of great churches that are doing amazing things in the areas of social justice, poverty and hunger initiatives, homeless ministry, and community engagement. I applaud those efforts and embrace the idea that the love of Christ has to be expressed in tangible and loving ways. But such efforts cannot negate the need to carefully cultivate relationships that go deep and offer real, substantive conversations about faith in Jesus Christ.

Let me illustrate this concept. For a number of years, I led congregations to participate in Habitat for Humanity building projects. Through the years we helped to build a number of homes and were glad to celebrate the families who were able to enjoy decent, affordable, and safe housing, many for the first time. But here's what I always found difficult to understand. Typically, in the areas where we built homes, several homes were being constructed up and down the same street. It was not unusual to have four or five going up at once. Our church worked on one, while a group of bank employees worked on another, while a team from a local university worked on yet another. Here was the troubling question that I always raised in my own mind and sometimes even in my sermons: "What was different about what we did as a group of committed Christians as opposed to what the other groups did?" All the groups hammered nails, cut wood, and painted walls. Did it make a difference that we worked under the idea that we were doing our thing "to the glory of God"? In reality, the answer is no; there isn't much difference. The difference is in the extra effort needed to build a long-term relationship with the family so that through the relationship, we could one day talk about Jesus. We need to be reminded that we are in the disciple-making business and not just construction workers. We need to become more deliberate with our message and purpose.[1]

Please don't misunderstand my thoughts about faith-sharing. Everyone needs to feel led by the Spirit to share his/her faith in the ways God prods them to act. Just as evangelism can be too "over the top," it can also be too low of a priority. It should never surprise a church when someone walks the aisle; it should surprise them when someone doesn't. My point is that the creation of relational space must become a priority in the ministry of every congregation if the desire is to fulfill the great commission. Churches do not exist to simply entertain the masses on Sunday or feed the hungry on Monday. They exist, first and foremost, to lead others into a saving knowledge of Jesus Christ. And that is done most effectively through genuine, honest, and loving relationships.

A final word on creating relational space. Don't wait on a relationship to come to you. Don't expect a newcomer to do all the work. Don't assume that someone is going to walk into your world and say, "I want to meet you and share life with you." You will be waiting a long time. Instead, take some initiative. Risk a little. Reach out. Create the space, and start a conversation. There is no limit on the number of relationships that your heart can hold. As long as there are people who are struggling, hurting, lost, panicked, broken, or lonely, you have a lot of space yet to create.

Endnote

[1] Before you read this and think too critically of the congregations I served, please know there were several from our team who went above and beyond the home-building requirements and established more permanent relationships with the new owners. Habitat for Humanity, by the way, continues to have my full support.

Chapter Four

Redemptive Space

Redemptive space is the whole reason we should strive to create any kind of space at all. It is the goal, the direction, the purpose of our pursuits. In fact, the key to any loving relationship is to help the other person find healing, wholeness, wellness, and joy. It's part of the reason we were placed on the planet. Consider for a moment the redemptive work of God. He creates space for us and enters into a relationship with us through Christ because he longs to redeem us, heal us, restore us. Truth be told, most of us struggle with broken-ness. As Paul predicted in Scripture long before any of us were created, we have missed the mark. We have chosen disobedience. We have failed to live up to the standards created for us. We have all sinned and fallen short of the glory of God (Rom 3:23). We feel the guilt and lean into the shame. We view ourselves like the broken toys of a child who has too many other objects with which to play. Once broken, we wallow in our self-loathing and pity and convince ourselves that God has abandoned and discarded us, and justifiably so. But that's where our understanding of God has gotten a little off the rails.

Listen to this simple but extremely important verse: "For God did not send his Son into the world to be its judge, but to be its savior" (John 3:17 GNT). God didn't create you with some sadistic intent to one day destine you to an eternal existence without him.

Just the opposite. God created you so he might enjoy time with you forever. Don't forget that you are his beloved. He sent his only son to die for your sins so you would not have to experience a pointless and eternal life of suffering. He longs to heal your brokenness, cleanse you of your sins, and claim you as his very own. He will not abandon you, discard you, or remove you from his list of favorites, no matter how messed up you believe yourself to be. You are never to be discarded, because you have ultimate worth as his child: "Know that the LORD is God. It is he who made us, and we are his; we are his people, the sheep of his pasture" (Ps 100:3 NIV).

If God's goal is that of creating redemptive relationships, then shouldn't ours be the same? Shouldn't we hope to form friendships that move from simple, surface conversations and interactions to those that go deep and actually bring some type of solace to those with whom we interact? Let's be clear about something. We are not the savior of the world, not even close. But we do represent him. And if we are open to the idea, he can work through us, offering words of counsel, insight, and wisdom that just may help to unburden the life of a friend who is struggling. Can we, in the pattern of our Savior, create the kind of welcoming, inviting, comforting space that will make a difference? Let's look at a couple examples from the pages of Luke's Gospel that help to tell the story of Jesus' power to reclaim the lost and heal the broken:

> Soon afterward Jesus went with his disciples to the village of Nain, and a large crowd followed him. A funeral procession was coming out as he approached the village gate. The young man who had died was a widow's only son, and a large crowd from the village was with her. When the Lord saw her, his heart overflowed with compassion. "Don't cry!" he said.

Then he walked over to the coffin and touched it, and the bearers stopped. "Young man," he said, "I tell you, get up." Then the dead boy sat up and began to talk! And Jesus gave him back to his mother.

Great fear swept the crowd, and they praised God, saying, "A mighty prophet has risen among us," and "God has visited his people today." And the news about Jesus spread throughout Judea and the surrounding countryside. (Luke 7:11–17 NLT)

This is an amazing story of resurrection that actually involves the lives of two different individuals for whom life was over. The first is obvious. A "young man" had passed away—from what circumstances we don't know. All we know is that when Jesus came upon the scene, the boy's mother and a sizable crowd from the city were grieving his loss. His body was broken, and his life energy was gone. The second person surrounded by the arms of death was the mother, a widow. To be a widow in the first-century world was to be an outcast. It meant social isolation. It meant poverty and sometimes prostitution. It meant she was powerless, defenseless, and vulnerable. The only hope of a widow for any sense of protection and normalcy was through the life of a son. Her identity, her worth and value, and her hope of any quality of life were bound to his existence, but now he was gone. It was such a moment of grief, fear, and loss. Not only had his life ended, but for all practical purposes, her life was ending as well. Surely those who gathered mourned the loss of both mother and child.

But notice the redeeming work of Jesus. First, he sees and understands the "moment in time." He sees deeply into her heart, into the depth of her grief, into the hopeless void that fills her life. Moved with compassion, he simply says to her, "Do not weep." How could such a word be given to a woman in such anguish? All she could possibly do is weep. There was nothing left to do, no hope to which to cling, no son for whom to care, no life still to be lived. But being moved by her brokenness, Jesus begins the restoration of life. He walks up and touches the coffin, and "the bearers stopped." It is not his physical hand on the coffin that makes them freeze in their tracks but rather the audacity of it all. Here was a Jewish rabbi, fluent in the demands of the Law and the rules of ceremonial cleanliness, yet he reaches to touch the coffin. He would be defiled. He would be rendered unclean. He would be ridiculed for such a foolish action. But love trumps protocol. And with his voice, he commands the young man to arise. The young man sits up and begins to speak. Jesus "gives" him back to his mother. In restoring his life, he restores her life as well. And fear grips them all.

Jesus, who had the power to heal the lame and raise the dead to life, created the space for a miracle. He not only stopped the oncoming funeral procession, but his large entourage as well: two crowds of people—one filled with the exciting, joyful, hopeful connection to a miracle-working Savior; the other filled with grief-stricken, desolate folks connected to death and pain. The two crowds couldn't have been more different. The intersection of the processions was like that of light and darkness meeting in time and space. But in the stillness of the moment, a moment in which I suppose the silence was deafening, Jesus welcomed the widow into space— relational space—with him. And sharing both emotion and compassion with her, he reached not only into the coffin but into the broken heart of this mother and healed her in ways no one could ever have imagined.

Sometimes when we create the space for a relationship to grow, we create the space for a miracle. It is in those moments of deep relational equity that we have the potential of being most Christlike. If we are willing to represent him in such a moment, we have the resources of the kingdom at our disposal to bind up a wound, to heal brokenness, to raise to life again that which has died.

During the seventeen years I served as pastor at my last church, we broadcasted our morning worship services "live" each Sunday. We encouraged people, through the use of a number on the screen, to call our church for help and counseling. A lot of folks called seeking counsel, prayer, and forgiveness. A dedicated group of volunteers manned the phones each week. It was not unusual for some of the conversations to continue long after the service was over and the sanctuary was empty. I'm sure some of those conversations with our dedicated volunteers were far more important than the words I offered from the pulpit.

One particular week, a desperate and lost man, whose name was Mark, was channel-surfing on Sunday morning while staying in a cheap hotel in the Nashville area. His life story was complicated, filled with many difficult twists and turns. He had been raised in a family compound in Ohio by an abusive and dictatorial father. So extensive was the emotional, physical, and verbal abuse that at the age of eighteen, Mark literally dug under a fence and escaped, running for his life. He would eventually make his way to the West Coast. To survive, he turned to anyone or anything that would help make his past disappear. He was, of course, vulnerable to all kinds of threats. Addiction entered his life. His abuse of alcohol and drugs became excessive. In order to have the means with which to fuel his pain-dulling addictive behavior, he did anything he could to make enough money to pay for the next bottle or the next fix. He did things like dealing drugs, stealing cars, and offering himself as a male prostitute. He lost his health, his looks, and his hope. He contracted AIDS and soon lost every friend he had known. He landed in Nashville to take some experimental treatments in an attempt to save his life.

He saw our television program that morning and decided to call the number on the bottom of the screen. He had only one question on his heart and mind: "Could God possibly love someone like me, after all that I have done and after what I have become?" In God's providence and timing, his call was answered by a former career Southern Baptist missionary named Ruth, who possessed as much of the grace and spirit of our Lord as any person I have ever known. She didn't judge. She didn't condemn. She didn't get all "preachy" on him. She just started listening and sharing with him about the love of Christ. She talked about forgiveness and grace. She invited him to church repeatedly and offered to meet him at the door. He was hesitant. He didn't come the first week or the next or the next. But he kept calling and kept asking for Ruth. And then it happened. One day he walked in the door. It had been a slow process. It took him months to have the courage to show up and then to sit through a service and then to start asking questions after the sermon. Some days he wreaked of alcohol and cigarettes. Other days he was a little more "put together." Our congregation drew him in. Collectively, we talked about grace and not judgment. (He even wrote a poem about me titled "The Preacher with a Smile.") It took a while, but eventually he began to discover grace. He even joined the church, and I had the honor of baptizing him into God's kingdom. He later moved to Florida for further treatment, where he died at the age of forty-nine.

Truth be told, Ruth saved his life—not physically, but emotionally and spiritually. She saved him through her words, her listening ear, and her compassionate, non-judgmental heart. By the way, she did the same thing with many others. But that's what redemptive space and the people filling it resembles. They listen. They don't judge. They offer hope. They hold hands. They cry. They love unconditionally. They point to an abundant life in Christ that is freeing, joyful, and unshackled to the past. It's the space every Christ-follower needs to create with whomever God brings to their doorstep. It's the kind of space every church needs to create if it desires to be a tangible expression of the kingdom of God on earth.

We often hear the words of 1 Corinthians 13 recited at weddings. After all, it's the "love chapter," right? To use it for a wedding ceremony is to somewhat co-opt its meaning and context. The descriptive words about love were not written by Paul to two young people promising their lives to each other. Instead, they were written to a church that was struggling to hold it all together. The unifying glue that would hold the church together was love. Unconditional love. Think about Paul's words in that context. And as you read them, consider what they say about creating redemptive space within the context of a congregation longing to represent Christ in its setting: "Love is patient and kind. Love is not jealous or boastful or proud or rude. It does not demand its own way. It is not irritable, and it keeps no record of being wronged. It does not rejoice about injustice but rejoices whenever the truth wins out. Love never gives up, never loses faith, is always hopeful, and endures through every circumstance" (1 Cor 13:4–7 NLT).

I don't know about you, but I would love to be connected to a church that practices radical hospitality and works hard at creating redemptive space to reclaim the lost, heal the broken, and restore the shattered. What if the spirit of our churches across the country was one of a patient, kind, forgiving, and hope-filled love? What if every nook and cranny, every Sunday school class, every small group, every conversation, every ministry endeavor, and every sanctuary felt like redemptive space? I suspect that the church-study "experts" would have no more reason to talk about "precipitous decline" among our membership. We wouldn't be able to build space fast enough to welcome the newcomers.

Here's the second story from the Gospel of Luke that describes the power of Christ to reclaim the lost and heal the broken. It's an amazing parable of Jesus used to describe the redemptive space created by a father who longs to see wholeness invade the life of a lost and wayward son. It's actually the story of two brothers and what can happen when redemptive space is claimed and when it is not. And it's actually our story as well. Let's first look at the story of the younger son.

> A man had two sons. The younger son told his father, "I want my share of your estate now before you die." So his father agreed to divide his wealth between his sons.

> A few days later this younger son packed all his belongings and moved to a distant land, and there he wasted all his money in wild living. About the time his money ran out, a great famine swept over the land, and he began to starve. He persuaded a local farmer to hire him, and the man sent him into his fields to feed the pigs. The young man became so hungry that even the pods he was feeding the pigs looked good to him. But no one gave him anything.

> When he finally came to his senses, he said to himself, "At home even the hired servants have food enough to spare, and here I am dying of hunger! I will go home to my father and say, 'Father, I have sinned against both heaven and you, and I am no longer worthy of being called your son. Please take me on as a hired servant.'"

So he returned home to his father. And while he was still a long way off, his father saw him coming. Filled with love and compassion, he ran to his son, embraced him, and kissed him. His son said to him, "Father, I have sinned against both heaven and you, and I am no longer worthy of being called your son."

But his father said to the servants, "Quick! Bring the finest robe in the house and put it on him. Get a ring for his finger and sandals for his feet. And kill the calf we have been fattening. We must celebrate with a feast, for this son of mine was dead and has now returned to life. He was lost, but now he is found." So the party began. (Luke 15:11–24)

There are elements of this story that are hard to even believe. First, consider the brazen audacity of the younger son to ask for his share of the estate. As the second-born son, he would have been entitled to one-third of his father's possessions, which he would have received upon his father's death. But with a petulant, "I-don't-want-to-wait" attitude, he asked for his portion. In a stunning move the father gives both money and independence to his child. And in no time flat, he packs up his stuff and hits the road, with his father's money, his father's reputation, his father's willingness, and his father's grieving fear all on his back. And it doesn't go well. You know the story. When the money runs out, so do the friends. Hunger drives him to a despicable job and to an unbearable existence. He finally remembers the joy of living in his father's presence, and with a well-rehearsed speech in his mind, he turns toward home.

It's also hard to believe what he finds when his feet hit the well-worn path at the gate that leads to his father's house. Ever since he walked away into the distant horizon, his father has been longing for his return. Each day, he strained his eyes against the rising sun to stare off into the distance, never giving up hope that his boy would return. And as soon as the father recognizes the skinny boy slowly walking up the path, with tears of joy streaking down the deep lines of his well-tanned face, he runs out to reclaim his child. It is not a scene of judgment, but grace. Not a scene of anger, but joy. Not a scene of rejection, but acceptance. He rushes to his son and embraces him with knee-trembling, lump-in-the-throat, voice-cracking joy. A party is thrown together, and the broken son is healed, welcomed, and reclaimed. It is the best of stories, and we would do well to tell it a thousand times over.

The redemptive space was created years earlier. It was created by a father's love. It was forged on the anvil of a long relationship, many conversations, and physical space within the father's house. The son chose to come home because he knew there was a home toward which he could turn. There are many whose names could be written into this story. Maybe even yours. It's the story of stubborn rebellion, foolish choices, and hard-to-believe grace. It is a story that all Christians need to know, tell, and live. We write ourselves into the narrative when we learn to forgive and forget, when we learn to listen and not judge, when we learn to embrace and not shun, when we create a space where the lost and broken are willing to inhabit. Remember that physical space leads to conversational space, which leads to relational space, which hopefully becomes redemptive space.

The work of creating redemptive space is not easy. It is messy, heartbreaking at times, disappointing at others, costly in both emotional and financial expense. It requires giving your life away so someone else can reclaim theirs. I have a friend named Jonas (not his real name). Jonas had a successful young life. He had friends in high school, was afforded a college education, had a nice car to drive, and plenty of women to enjoy. In college he was introduced to a different lifestyle than he had known while growing up. The party crowd taught him to drink and try drugs and even gamble a bit. There were a lot of excesses in his life that extended well beyond college. When school was over, he got a good job and made some real money. He was popular, friendly, and somewhat responsible. But the high life continued to take advantage of Jonas until it overtook him. He partied. He abused substances. He spent money—a lot of it. The company where he worked had to close, and Jonas was left without a job, but with few worries. There was plenty of money to support his lifestyle, or so he thought. He bought tickets to ball games, bought lots of drugs, and befriended a lot of bookies. He was hooked by any number of dangerous connections. And then his world came crashing down. He vividly remembers going to an ATM and seeing this message for the first time: "insufficient funds."

His life began a downward spiral. He lost his car, his apartment, his friends, his self-esteem. But he found the church—our church— and things began to turn around. We gave him food to eat and a place to stay. We helped him manage his debts and find a new job. He got settled into a rental house he could afford and bought a car to drive. He got involved in a recovery group. What I didn't know was that all the while we were helping him, he was lying to us. He was still using. Still betting. Still making bad choices. It all came crashing down on a weekend I will long remember. He and his drug dealer had been "using" all night. The police were called to the house, where they found too much paraphernalia to ignore. He was arrested. And while handcuffed in the back seat of police cruiser, he asked the police to call one of our deacons and me. The deacon and I talked about what to do. We decided not to try some costly and enabling action. With broken hearts we had to say, "Let him go to jail." It was one of those tough love moments that we hoped and prayed would be life-changing and life-saving.

He spent a week in jail. It was brutally frightening for all of us. The phone calls were desperate. Behind the scenes we worked with law enforcement officials, judges, and attorneys. We were able to get some charges dropped and arrange for some community service rather than more time in jail. The day he was released, the first place he wanted to go was to our church. I remember the reunion. We hugged and cried and talked for hours. I talked to him about grace and second chances and making better choices. He was broken, but he knew we would help him find healing. He found a place of welcome in the Father's house. He was not condemned, but loved. Not forgotten, but embraced. Not ignored, but included. His redemption eventually led to a place of leadership in our church. To this day he serves as a deacon in that congregation, leads a recovery group, and welcomes everyone who walks in the door on Sunday morning. You should hear his testimony (but get comfortable— you will be there for a while!). Redemptive space declares, "You are welcome here, Jonas. We value who you are rather than judge what you have been. Let's heal and grow together as brothers and sisters in Christ."

But back to Jesus's parable. There is another son to consider. He too had choices to make. And certainly one of them was whether or not to create redemptive space in his world to welcome his lost brother. Here's his story:

> Meanwhile, the older son was in the fields working.
> When he returned home, he heard music and dancing
> in the house, and he asked one of the servants what
> was going on. "Your brother is back," he was told,
> "and your father has killed the fattened calf. We are
> celebrating because of his safe return."

The older brother was angry and wouldn't go in. His father came out and begged him, but he replied, "All these years I've slaved for you and never once refused to do a single thing you told me to. And in all that time you never gave me even one young goat for a feast with my friends. Yet when this son of yours comes back after squandering your money on prostitutes, you celebrate by killing the fattened calf!"

His father said to him, "Look, dear son, you have always stayed by me, and everything I have is yours. We had to celebrate this happy day. For your brother was dead and has come back to life! He was lost, but now he is found!" (Luke 15:25–32 NLT)

Sadly, the rest of the story is reflective of a different attitude and approach. The older son—overtaken by anger, resentment, and judgment—fails to welcome his brother home. He is willing to let the distance caused by brokenness remain. His abusive cynicism breaks his father's heart. Remember that everything once owned by the father is now owned by the older son. All the land, the cattle, the structures, the servants, and even the possessions were his. The father had granted them to the oldest son on the same day he gave the younger son his portion: "Everything I have is yours" (v. 31). Nothing about his inheritance would be affected by welcoming his brother home again. He has absolutely nothing to lose. But he can add to the father's joy by respecting his example and following his lead. The story ends with the father begging the oldest boy to join in the celebration. We are not told how he responds.

It is also our unending story. Life will constantly provide us with opportunities to create redemptive space. We will have ample opportunity to extend grace to the fallen or to offer judgment.

We can be like our Father. We can heal the broken, forgive the sin, bind up the wound, restore the reputation, and reclaim the lost. Or we can stand on the outskirts of grace and just listen from the outside to the sound of those who live in joy while our dark humanity squeezes out the last joy from our hearts. It was not the younger son who lost his way—not at all. It was the older son and many others like him who refuse to let the hurting come home again. When you are faced with the choice of grace or judgment, always choose grace.

I'm not Catholic, but I know a few things about the Catholic faith, including a priority on confession of sin. In my limited understanding of the process, here's how it works: Someone who has committed a sin is convicted by the Holy Spirit to repent of such action and confess the sin. In Catholic practice the confession is made to the priest in the privacy and confidentiality of the confessional booth. It begins with a contrite heart that is willing to name one's sins, no matter how grievous or how frequently committed. The sinner steps into the confession booth, where he/she offers the confession to the priest. The priest then offers grace to the sinner through some form of absolution or penance. Though Catholics and mainline Protestants may disagree with the priest's role in the process, all Christ-followers should recognize the importance of confessing sin and the healing that occurs when the confession is heartfelt. May I suggest that the confession booth represents redemptive space? The wounded and weary find a safe place in which they can unburden their lives. There, they find a gentle grace and liberating forgiveness.

What if each of us could learn how to create such a place of welcome, non-judgment, helpful thoughts and prayers, and listening compassion in the places where we live? What if each of us was willing to invest deeply in the lives of others? What if we were willing to give away some of our lives in order to help others reclaim a little of theirs? The creation of such space is deliberate, willful, and time-consuming. It takes acceptance. It takes careful attention. It takes listening. It takes compassion. It takes a non-judgmental spirit. It takes investment. The progression of a casual conversation to a redemptive, healing conversation might take months or even years. Relational equity is not easily created. But once it is, it can be most rewarding to those who are in relationship with each other. The goal of redemptive space is not to tolerate, accept, or sanction someone's poor choices or past mistakes. It is not about creating a surface-level, "feel-good-about-yourself" moment. It's about the hard work of taking a broken aspect of someone's life and helping them find a healing balm. It's about bridging separation. It's about swapping self-loathing for a healthy self-loving reality. It's about turning bitterness into joy and shame into esteem. It's about teaching someone to speak a new language of hope and renewal rather than the abusive words of shame and sorrow. It's about helping others view their lives through the lens of Christ's grace and redemptive work. The creation of such space should receive the best of our efforts.

Singer/songwriter Pat Terry has a song about forgiveness on his album *Laugh for a Million Years*.[1] The song is simply titled "Forgiveness." Here are some of the lyrics:

> In that dark swift river called love,
> down on the bottom so deep and cold,
> there lies a healing stone, worn smooth from the water's flow.
> It's a beautiful thing to behold. It took years for the river to make. God even gave it a name, forgiveness.
> It will heal a lot of hurt along the way, it can take a grievous wound and bind it, dry your tears and soothe away the pain. Forgiveness.

I like so much about of the imagery of his words. I also appreciate the fact that sometimes the "healing stone" takes years to create. I am reminded that this work of creating redemptive space can be a long, drawn-out, difficult endeavor. But when we dare to create it, it can, in Terry's words, "heal a lot of hurt along the way, it can take a grievous wound and bind it, dry your tears and soothe away the pain." To be sure *forgiveness* is not the only word that needs to be discussed in the context of redemptive space, but it is certainly at the heart of most of the brokenness that is found in such a place. I invite you to go deep and find the place in your relationship with a friend where you not only offer the words of Christ, but where you, in fact, become the essence of all that he is.

Endnote

[1] Pat Terry, "Forgiveness," *Laugh for a Million Years*, Horse and Sandwich Records (January 2010).

Chapter Five

Reflective Space

⌒𝒢

I wrote the following words in the introduction to this book: "Reflective space is the private space that we need to carve out for ourselves. Each of us needs time to meditate, reflect, ponder, wonder, and rest. We need time for our thoughts to meander a little. We need the space to ask ourselves, 'What does this mean? How does this impact my life? What is God seeking to do in this place? What does he want me to do with this moment?'" Reflective space is all about introspection, growth, and wisdom. It's the quiet space where we learn, reflect, and grow. This space may be the most difficult to create, because it involves introspection, time, and self-honesty. It may force us to see things in ourselves that we don't want to see, or even more so, it may cause us to discover the things yet unseen about ourselves and about our journey. We may discover paths that God wants us to take, places he wants us to explore, and lives he wants us to engage. Reflective space, though quiet and pensive, often leads to more involvement and a greater call to give away self.

Gospel writer Mark helps us to see Jesus and his sense of the importance of reflective space. Take the following story recorded in Mark 4:

> As evening came, Jesus said to his disciples, "Let's cross to the other side of the lake." So they took Jesus in the boat and started out, leaving the crowds

behind (although other boats followed). But soon a fierce storm came up. High waves were breaking into the boat, and it began to fill with water.

Jesus was sleeping at the back of the boat with his head on a cushion. The disciples woke him up, shouting, "Teacher, don't you care that we're going to drown?"

When Jesus woke up, he rebuked the wind and said to the waves, "Silence! Be still!" Suddenly the wind stopped, and there was a great calm. Then he asked them, "Why are you afraid? Do you still have no faith?"

The disciples were absolutely terrified. "Who is this man?" they asked each other. "Even the wind and waves obey him!" (Mark 4:35–41 NLT)

There are a couple observations to make. First, consider what precedes this story in the text. According to Mark the day had been spent preaching and teaching "a very large crowd" (4:1 NASB) that had gathered on the hillside by the sea. In fact, the crowd was so large that Jesus got in a boat, pushed away from the shore, and taught the people while sitting in the boat. He taught them many things through the use of parables. Presumably, the teaching went on throughout the day and even into the evening. So after a long, exhausting day of preaching, Jesus suggested that he and the disciples cross over to the other side of the lake. Sometimes we all need a little space to be alone with our thoughts.

Jesus was setting some boundaries around his life and ministry. He knew that the exhaustion of the day needed a little solitude and rest to counteract it. He carved out both the time and the space for a little "downtime." Jesus separated himself from the crowds and forced himself to rest. If there was any doubt about his physical exhaustion, notice what happens next: He falls asleep on a cushion in the stern of the boat, in the middle of the sea, in the middle of twelve anxious men, in the middle of a huge storm. Such storms were not uncommon. Because of the topography of the region, it was not unusual for winds to become funneled through the mountains and spill out onto the sea. A calm day could become a raging storm in a relatively short period of time. The disciples, fearful for their very lives, shake him awake and ask, "Do you not care that we are perishing?" Rising to his feet, he speaks to the storm, saying, "Hush! Be still." Suddenly, the winds abate; surely the disciples' raging fear dissipates as well.

That's the second observation from this story: the calming of a restless soul. Part of creating reflective space requires a willingness on our part to allow the swirling winds of stress and worry to dissipate. Reflective space gives us time to think rationally, pray carefully, and step positively into our thoughts of angst. We need to let the raging seas calm a little. We need perspective. We need insight. We need wisdom. We need positive steps to take. Reflective space allows us to speak calm into some of the fears and worries we face. It's the deep breath, the step back, the contemplative thought. Such moments won't come without deliberate and conscious choices to make them happen.

There was a time in my personal ministry when I was a little overburdened. I didn't recognize it then, but I do now. For several years on end, this was my weekly routine: I wrote and prepared two sermons for Sunday, developed a Wednesday night Bible study, taught class three days a week at a university, led a Thursday night Bible study, and sometimes taught a Sunday school lesson as well. In case you lost track, that was eight teaching/preaching preparations every week. Reflective space was never created. I just kept plowing ahead in order to feed the machinery of ministry. (If you have ever served a local church as a pastor, you recognize such an experience.) Reflective space would have made me a better scholar, a better preacher, and certainly a better pastor and head of household. But the storms we create with our busyness rage on, and we hang on for dear life until something forces us to rest. Unfortunately, for most ministers the rest comes in the form of burnout or compassion fatigue.

Here's a second story from Mark's Gospel that illustrates what can happen when we inhabit reflective space:

> Immediately after this, Jesus insisted that his disciples get back into the boat and head across the lake to Bethsaida, while he sent the people home. After telling everyone good-bye, he went up into the hills by himself to pray.
>
> Late that night, the disciples were in their boat in the middle of the lake, and Jesus was alone on land. He saw that they were in serious trouble, rowing hard and struggling against the wind and waves. About three o'clock in the morning Jesus came toward them, walking on the water. He intended to go past them, but when they saw him walking on the water, they cried out in terror, thinking he was a ghost. They were all terrified when they saw him.
>
> But Jesus spoke to them at once. "Don't be afraid," he said. "Take courage! I am here!" Then he climbed into the boat, and the wind stopped. They were totally amazed, for they still didn't understand the

significance of the miracle of the loaves. Their hearts
were too hard to take it in. (Mark 6:45–52 NLT)

This passage begins with the phrase "Immediately after this." It's crucial to understand the context. This story of Jesus sending the crowds away and walking on the sea follows the telling of the story of the feeding of the 5,000. The miracle event and story that follows it is told by all four Gospel writers. (The feeding of the 5,000 is the only miracle, by the way, recorded in all four Gospels.). Notice that after another long day of teaching and working miracles, Jesus understands the value of going away alone for an evening to pray. He needs the space, the respite, the moment to reflect. The disciples are sent on ahead. They venture onto the sea with the intention of reaching the other side sometime during the night. The assumption is that Jesus would catch up later. The text mentions that Jesus is "alone on the land." In the wee hours of the morning, Jesus is able to see the disciples and perceive the trouble they encounter. Understand that the disciples are miles away from Jesus at this point in the narrative. With supernatural ability he is able to see them straining against the wind and waves.

Here's the takeaway from that passage: Because Jesus allowed himself to inhabit reflective space, he was able to see the disciples in their time of peril. Reflective space provides such perspective. When we allow ourselves time to slow down, get quiet, and carefully process all that swirls around in our lives, we begin to see with greater clarity. We see ourselves and others more clearly. We recognize the trauma, the stress, the pain, and the unsettling fears in others' lives. We see more. We understand more. And we begin to consider ways to help. It's the same for our own lives. Reflective space allows us to see ourselves more clearly. The pause, the recess, the timeout allows us the time and distance to process, consider, learn, and grow.

When I celebrated my tenth anniversary as pastor at my previous church, the congregation graciously gave me a month-long paid sabbatical. There were no stipulations on how to use the time. It was to be personal time during which I could travel, read, fish, golf, hang out with friends, etc. It was a unique experience. I noticed after the first week that I found myself missing meals. I would just forget to eat! The reason? I wasn't ever hungry. It dawned on me that I was churning through so much activity and stress in my day-to-day job that I *had* to eat in order to give my body the energy it needed to keep up the pace. When the stress was gone, my metabolism slowed considerably. I was also fascinated by my approach to work and ministry at the end of the sabbatical period. I came back refreshed, recharged, and excited to get going again. Many in the congregation noticed the change, and several suggested that my preaching showed greater depth and more passion once I returned. Why? Because of the reflective space.[1]

Consider for a moment the life of King David, who is considered to be the greatest king of Israel. There were so many stellar moments, so many victories, so many great days. But there was also that whole episode with Bathsheba (2 Sam 11). I don't know at what point in his life David had a moment of reflective time to consider the consequences of his action, but I believe that such a moment came. The reflective space allowed him to see his own sinfulness, his failed morality, and the distance created between himself and God. It also gave him the time and energy needed to claim repentance and seek God in new and powerful ways. Consider just a portion of Psalm 51, in which David pours out his heart of repentance:

> Hide Your face from my sins
> And blot out all my iniquities.
> Create in me a clean heart, O God,

And renew a steadfast spirit within me.
Do not cast me away from Your presence
And do not take Your Holy Spirit from me.
Restore to me the joy of Your salvation
And sustain me with a willing spirit.
Then I will teach transgressors Your ways,
And sinners will be converted to You. (Ps 51:9–13
NASB)

There is much to be said for a long period of soul-searching, in which we question our actions, our motivations, and our attitudes. But more than seeking some solace for past mistakes, the reflective space also allows room for God to tap on our shoulder or whisper in our ear. You've known such moments—moments when God longs to impart a new direction and purpose in your life. Without the quiet space, how will we ever hear God's "still, small voice"?

At times, reflective space can welcome a visitor. By that, I mean it is okay to include others in the process of evaluation and reflective thinking. In fact, it is often vital to connect with godly individuals who can help to affirm, clarify, or even suggest what God may be longing to impart. Our own opinions, thoughts, and preconceived notions often have a way of blurring the lines of communication. A seasoned, mature voice can be a critical piece of the discernment process. But let's be clear—the work of reflective space is primarily a personal discipline. Though we may call on others to gain perspective, those individuals cannot become a crutch on which we constantly lean in hearing from God and making our decisions.

Journaling can help create reflective space. If you are like me, it helps to write things down. A moment of insight, a thought, or a word of discernment can often be lost in the whirlwind of activity that swirls around our daily lives. There is something important about the process of writing such things in a journal, where you can recall the thought process and even refine the message. I write sermon notes, Bible study material, illustrations, and even meanderings in those pages. To put pencil to paper forces me to process the thoughts and give them expression. It also gives me a way to collect and keep such meditations, lest I lose them to the sands of time and a distracted mind.

Sometimes even churches need reflective space. Most congregations get into ruts and routines, though not all of them are bad. Some of the routines are productive, and some even foster great ministry opportunities. But most of them are the result of a "that's-the-way-we've-always-done-it" mentality. Years ago, in his book *The Purpose Driven Church*, Pastor Rick Warren asked faith leaders to consider the following question: "If your church was not already doing a particular ministry, would it start it now?"[2] It was a way of saying that careful and periodic evaluation needs to happen in the life of any church.

The times, they are a-changin'. The church is tasked with the responsibility of trying to offer relevance, reverence, and relationship to people blown about by the ever-shifting winds of culture. Some ministries and programming are no longer productive. Far too many congregations are stuck in traditional habits and systems that are no longer working. Churches need to stop, look, and listen. They need to create the space as a body to evaluate current programming and staffing. They need to look around community and culture and decide what needs to happen. Churches need to consider what needs to change, what needs to be tossed aside, and what needs to find new life. The work of the kingdom is far too vital to ignore the creation of reflective space.

What does that resemble in the life of a local church ministry? First, it looks like contemplative worship moments. So often we fill our worship services up to the brim with songs, sermons, and sayings. What we often lack are moments for people to actually reflect on what God might be revealing to them in such a moment. For years, those of us who led worship tacked on the invitation at the end of the service as though it was some sort of afterthought. In reality, it should be the pivotal moment in which people can respond to the promptings of God that have been experienced in word and worship. I also wonder if it might help to offer a guided contemplative moment near the beginning of a worship experience. What if the worship leader offered a "road map" as to where worship was headed and how one might hear a word from the Lord? In other words, what if participants had a moment to anticipate God's presence? Could such a moment of quiet grace give greater depth to the experience?

The last three churches I pastored all televised their services. There was always a self-imposed pressure to fill every minute with something, anything. The goal was not to have any "dead time" in our television broadcast. It may have made for good television, but it was bad for worship. We robbed ourselves of reflective space that could have been a vital portion of worship each week.

Second, periodic retreats can be extremely meaningful, both corporately and individually. Groups within a congregation can benefit by having some time away to rest, reflect, and rethink. Retreats become the comma we place in the busy life of the church, providing the membership with sufficient time to ask questions about purpose, core values, and ministry initiatives. Churches would also do well to encourage members to retreat as individuals. Rather than pack a weekend full with games, conferences, and activities, what would it be like to have thirty people spend most of the weekend relaxing at a retreat setting? They could read, think, and pray, and then gather at the end of each day to reflect collectively and to discern the ways in which God is at work.

Third, reflective space could even mean the intentional lessening of programming for a season, all for the purpose of careful thinking. What if, for a semester, a lot of the non-essential programs and activities ceased in order to give folks a break from the torrid pace of church life? Could a church intentionally "scale down" for a few months in order to discern new direction and new initiatives? Would such a discipline help churches ensure every bit of "ministry energy" was being used purposefully? A lot of what we do in church may have more to do with entertaining the masses and less to do with building the kingdom. Reflective space might allow us to discern the difference.

I grew up working on cars. Our driveway was always filled with British sportscars. My dad had a passion for them, so my brother and I developed the same passion. We owned MGs, Triumphs, Austin Healeys, and the like. We changed oil, rotated tires, fixed clutches, and even pulled an engine on occasion. To this day I still like to tinker a little under the hood. Sometimes working on a car can be a frustrating experience. Sometimes a bolt won't loosen, a part won't fit, or a screw gets stripped. It's easy to get stressed or maybe even a little angered by it all. But here's what I have discovered along the way: Sometimes when a part just doesn't seem to fit correctly or a bolt won't line up, it helps to walk away for a few minutes. I can't really explain it, but on many occasions, as soon as I began working again after some time away, whatever was so frustrating suddenly became an easy task.

Sometimes we need to "walk away"—from our ministry pursuits, our occupations, our involvements, even our noble efforts—long enough to reflect on what we are doing and why we are doing those things. We may find a greater passion for our work, a better path to success, or a clearer understanding of God's purpose and direction for our lives. Neglect the reflective space, and you just might spend your life in frustration and longing, with nothing of value to show for your work.

I hope you will consider the challenge to carve out the time and distance needed to create reflective space in your own life. Like viewing the stars on a clear night from a distant pasture, where the distracting lights of the city can't find you, reflective space may allow you to see yourself, your journey, and God's plan a little more clearly. All of us are being written into God's greater narrative. Take a little time to reflect, and you just might catch a glimpse of the movement of his pen.

Endnotes

[1] As a side note, if your church does not have a sabbatical plan in place for all staff ministers, it is doing itself and those ministers no favors. Periodic sabbaticals will lead to greater effectiveness and longevity.

[2] Rick Warren, *The Purpose Driven Church* (Grand Rapids: Zondervan, 1995).

Conclusion

During a conversation with his disciples just hours before his arrest in the garden, Jesus offered these words: "Do not let your heart be troubled; believe in God, believe also in Me. In My Father's house are many dwelling places; if it were not so, I would have told you; for I go to prepare a place for you. If I go and prepare a place for you, I will come again and receive you to Myself, that where I am, there you may be also. And you know the way where I am going" (John 14:1–4 NASB).

The image behind Jesus's words is that of a bridegroom preparing a place for his bride. In the days of the first century, nuclear families became extended families, yet without leaving home. It was the practice of the day for a son to continue to live in his father's household even after marriage. Once engaged, the son would begin the process of building a room or multiple rooms onto his father's house. Once the room or rooms were complete, he would retrieve his bride and bring her into their new home. Jesus uses that image to describe the place of welcome he is creating for all of us. We need not worry; there will be room for us all in God's forever kingdom. He is building the space and will call us home.

Hang on to the image of the son building rooms onto the father's house for a moment. Carefully, methodically, purposefully, he creates the space where he will carve out a life for himself and his wife. They will talk, eat, love, and live in that space. The relationship will flourish. The two of them will grow old together in that space.

Because we are made in the image of our Father, we have the ability to create space. We can create rooms for others to inhabit. We can carefully, methodically, and purposefully open our lives again and again. We really do have the ability to make space for things to happen, for lives to thrive, for relationships to bloom, and for people to find wholeness. Open your door. Open your mind. Open your ears. Open your heart. The space will become filled in glorious ways that you can't begin to imagine.

Afterthoughts

God Space

⟳

The principles outlined in this book can also be applied to the process of building a relationship with God. A recent conversation with a co-worker led to the following questions: "How can I go deeper with God? How can I invest more in a relationship with him that will actually make a difference in my life?" This co-worker admitted to me that she had grown up with a surface-level faith at best. Her faith tradition emphasized learning key doctrines and memorizing certain confessions rather than actually digging deeply into God's Word. She admitted that her faith experience suffered because of it. She felt as though she had known God from a distance, not as a loving Father with whom she could spend time each day. She wanted to learn more, explore more, and be drawn into a more vibrant, day-to-day, God-dependent faith. I began describing ways for her to develop a daily discipline of Scripture reading, thoughtful reflection, and prayer. Suddenly it clicked: I was asking her to create space with God in the same way I had written to encourage others about creating space with various people in their lives. So, if I may, allow me a few moments of reflection on creating God space.

It is vitally important to create physical space in your life to welcome God into your world. By suggesting the creation of physical space, I am literally encouraging you to create a moment, a place, and an open mind. It is important to create a moment with the Father. This needs to be a consistent moment, carved into each day, in which you allow yourself time to sit in his presence. For some, the "God moment" might best be created at the start of day. Before the house comes to life, the kids awaken, or the pressures of the job begin to infringe upon a potentially reflective moment, create a consistent time to interact with the Father through prayer, thoughtful reflection, and the reading of his Word. Maybe your best reflective moments come in the evening when the world has settled down and you can look back across the expanse of your day and consider where you have found God's presence in your life. Maybe in the stillness of the night, before your eyes close to rest, you can most consistently find moments to welcome God into your world. The creation of God space begins with a consistent moment.

God space also requires a consistent place. Most of us will do well to find an actual physical place in which we can spend moments with God each day. Where is that space that you can be alone? Where can you give yourself fully to your moments of reflection? It may be at the breakfast table where you sip your morning coffee before the rest of the house comes to life. It may be a corner table at a local coffee shop you tend to visit most days. It may be the well-worn leather recliner in your den. It may be the edge of your bed with your open Bible sitting on the nightstand. It could even be in your car, where you purposefully turn off both your phone and your radio so you can hear yourself think and listen for God to whisper. Place is important. You need to consider a place that offers you a consistent, uninterrupted moment.

God space also requires an open mind. We will learn little about God if we enter our God space with an agenda, an attitude, or a closed mind. We need to clear our heads of the worries that distract, the pressures that pull focus, and the well-entrenched opinions that keep us from learning something new. What if we truly stopped, looked, and listened for God to speak, to nudge, to inform, or to challenge us? An open mind allows his Spirit to give guidance and instruction. An open mind says we are willing to learn, to question, and to grow. An open mind is best formed when humility overtakes our humanity and we ask God to renew our thoughts, our motivations, and our hearts.

When I was a student at Samford University, I was required to take a drama appreciation course. I, along with the other students, learned about projecting my voice, making eye contact with the audience, and using appropriate gestures as I spoke. I'm not sure I would have ever made it as a great actor, but I appreciate the skills I was taught. What I remember most about the experience occurred one particular day in class. A senior drama major was enlisted to perform a soliloquy. I remember that she was dressed in costume and that she was quite eloquent with her words and diction. She was amazing, and we sat quiet and still, spellbound by her performance. The stage was completely dark except for a circle of bright light. When she stepped into the light, she came alive, and the performance took flight. She inhabited the space. She drew the focus completely to herself. No one thought of the darkness around her, the gentle buzzing of the stage lights, or the occasional squeaking of the seats. It was all about her presence in that defined spot.

It is my prayerful hope that we can create such a space for God—where the irrelevant world around us fades away, where the distractions cease, and where the light of his presence illuminates the stage. We have to be intentional about that space. We have to push away our stray thoughts, declutter our minds, and momentarily forget our overpacked schedules so we can be fully present with God. Create the space often enough, and you will soon escape the uncomfortable feeling of what it means to be still and quiet for a moment.

As I have described in this book, the physical space will lead to conversational space with the Father. If we spend enough time in his presence, a conversation will begin. Oh, it may not resemble the kind of conversation we have with others, where audible words are exchanged, but our conversations will create moments for us to be engaged, open, and gut-wrenchingly honest about who we are and what we have done. We will learn to pour out our hearts without pretense, without deception, and without the fear of condemnation. In those moments God will listen to our words and to our hearts. And we will hear from him as well. He may reveal himself with a word of revelation that emerges from the pages of his Word. He may speak through the words of a friend or family member. He may reveal himself with a gentle prodding of his Spirit or through a simple whisper of grace and guidance.

You know where the conversations will take you, right? A relationship will emerge. There will be depth. There will be insight. There will be peace of mind. There will be joy. There will be fellowship. We will go from the awkwardness of a new friendship to the welcome embrace of a lasting relationship. It won't happen overnight. Disciplines like Scripture reading, reflection, and journaling may begin as arduous tasks. But soon the careful discipline will become engaging discipleship. You will begin to see God as a loving Father, not an abuser. A king, not a tyrant. A friend, not an enemy. Your heart will change. Your priorities will shift. Your vision will sharpen. Your compassion will grow. You will know his heart, and he will know yours. And the changes that need to be made within you will be made with gentleness, kindness, and mercy. The relationship will become so meaningful that you will wonder how you ever survived apart from it—and then you will realize that there was never any real life without it.

The redemptive space created by the relationship will soon come into focus. Embraced in the arms of your Father, you will find healing, comfort, redemption, patience, and hope. You will find joy, not sorrow. Love, not anger. Peace, not turmoil. Blessing, not cursing. Acceptance, not rejection. Inclusion, not distance. In finding peace with God, you will also find peace with yourself. You will realize that you are loved beyond measure, forgiven beyond your wildest hope, and received into his family without qualification.

You may even realize for the first time that the space you thought you were creating for God was actually the discovery of the space he created for you to share with him long before you were ever born. You see, you don't have to invite God into your space—you have to allow yourself to enter into his. That space was created by a skilled carpenter more than 2,000 years ago. It's time you found it.